VOGUE GUIDE TO
Knitting

GALAHAD BOOKS • NEW YORK

Editor: Judy Brittain
Assistant Editor: Susan Read
Technical Editor: Pamela Dawson
Editor Condé Nast Books: Alex Kroll

Contents

Introduction	5
Abbreviations	7
Casting on	8
Knitting and purling	10
Basic stitches	12
Tension	14
Shaping	16
Patterned stitches	20
Lace stitches	24
Aran stitches	28
Fair Isle and tubular knitting	32
Knitting from a pattern	34
Making adjustments to patterns	36
Finishing touches	38
Making up knitted garments	44
Hints on care and washing	49
Embroidered jacket	50
Butterfly vest	52
Sequin jacket	54
Lace cardigan and skirt	56
Classic cable cardigan	59
Cardigans for beginners	60
His and her moss stitch sweater	63
Fair Isle pullovers	64
Aran sampler cardigan	66
Smock	69
Ribbed hat	71
Angora cardigans	71
Cap-sleeved sweaters	74
Cable bikini	76
Lace stitch bikini	78
Shawl and handbag	80
Gloves and socks	82
Child's cable sweater	84
Child's Fair Isle sweater and beret	86
Military coat with beret	88
Baby's shawl	90
Bedspread	92
Cushions	93
Doll with clothes	95
Yarn conversion chart	96

Acknowledgements: Drawings: Barbara Firth. Photographers: Karl Stoecker – Front cover and pages 50, 54, 57, 59, 62, 67, 69, 73, 77, 79, 83, 85. Stuart Brown – page 64. David Montgomery – pages 53, 86, 89. Peter Rand – pages 61, 90. John Wingrove – Back cover and pages 93, 94. Still life photography: Maurice Dunphy. Hair in Karl Stoecker photographs by Aaron Glynn of Freelancers.

Introduction

Knitting is an extremely ancient craft dating back to the Phoenician and Egyptian cultures. Each generation passed their knitting knowledge on to the next one and this method of learning continued right up to Victorian times. Then, with the start of ladies' journals, design instructions were printed and made available to a much wider audience. Since then knitters have become somewhat spoon-fed and have stopped making up their own designs, using instead the easier method of working from published instructions.

Recently there has been a revival of interest in all the hand crafts with a particularly strong focus on knitting. In this age of mass production, this interest stems primarily from the need to be able to create something oneself.

Vogue Guide to Knitting deals with all the aspects of hand-knitting. It includes designs for garments in the fashion shapes of today, as well as the new and elegant classics. There are also a large number of stitch samples, illustrating basic, Aran and lacy stitches, and Fair Isle techniques. It is hoped that readers will want to start designing their own patterns; the various stitches described can be worked to suit many styles. Also, by using different colour combinations, a classic round-necked sweater can become an original and beautiful design.

The possibilities of hand-knitting extend from clothing into the home, where rugs, bedspreads, cushions, table-cloths and even curtains can be made with beautiful results.

Detail of hand knitted wall hanging, French, late 18th-century, lent to the Victoria and Albert Museum by Mr E. W. Passold

Introduction

Types of yarns

'Yarn' is the collective name for threads which have been spun for knitting. These threads can consist of wool, cotton, nylon, silk, hair, flax, hemp, metals or numerous man-made fibres, all of which can be used alone or in various combinations. These strands are known to the spinners as 'counts' and they, in turn, make up a ply, 2, 3, 4 or more, which make up the yarn. A ply can be any number of strands or counts and does not necessarily refer to the thickness of the yarn. It is for this reason that it is not advisable to substitute one yarn for another when working from a pattern. A 2-ply can be thicker than a 3-ply, as is the case with Shetland or other home-spun yarns, and it is most important to use the particular yarn recommended for a design. The character of the yarn is deter-mined in the process known as 'doubling', which forms a workable knitting yarn. If the twist of the yarn is tight, it will knit up into a hard-wearing garment, and is suitable for men's pullovers, socks and outer garments. Looser twisted yarns are more suitable for babywear, undergarments and bedjackets. In the case of man-made fibre, used alone or in combination with wool, the yarn can be loose and yet very hard-wearing. Fancy doubling or twisting produces bouclés, knop yarns and tweed wools. The character of any yarn is always taken into account when planning a design and if the designer has stipulated a bouclé yarn, you will not obtain satisfactory results by using, say, a 4-ply crêpe quality.

Types of needles

Knitting needles can be made from many different materials—bone, wood, metal and plastics. Whatever the material used, they are made to a standard gauge in Britain. These range from the finest needles, graded as numbers 17, 16 and so on to the largest size, graded as number 1. Very large needles can also be obtained which are in sizes 0, 00 and 000, and in $\frac{1}{2}''$, $\frac{3}{4}''$ and $1''$ sizes. Knitting needles are usually sold in pairs, pointed at one end and with a knob at the other end to stop the stitches falling off; they come in varying lengths. Needles are also made as sets of four, pointed at both ends, and circular needles; these are used for knitting socks, and garments where a seam is not required.

In Europe and America a different method of grading is used. As an example, the British No 9 needle would be given as No $3\frac{1}{2}$ in France and No 4 in America (see chart).

When choosing your needles, make sure that they are long enough to hold your stitches without crowding, and that they are in a colour different from your yarn to avoid possible eye-strain.

Knitting needles

United Kingdom	000	00	0	1	2	3	4	5	6	7	8	9	10	11	12	13	14
United States	15	13	12	11	$10\frac{1}{2}$	10	9	8	7	6	5	4	3	2	1	0	00
Continental mm	9	$8\frac{1}{2}$	8	$7\frac{1}{2}$	7	$6\frac{1}{2}$	6	$5\frac{1}{2}$	5	$4\frac{1}{2}$	4	$3\frac{1}{2}$	$3\frac{1}{4}$	$3/2\frac{3}{4}$	$2\frac{1}{2}$	$2\frac{1}{4}$	2

Knitting abbreviations

alt	alternate
beg	begin(ing)
cont	continue(ing)
dec	decrease
foll	following
g-st	garter-stitch (every row knit)
inc	increase
k	knit
k up	pick up and knit
k-wise	knit wise
m 1	make one (pick up loop below next stitch and knit)
m-st	moss stitch
no(s)	number(s)
oz(s)	ounce(s)
psso	pass slipped stitch over
p2sso	pass two slipped stitches over
patt	pattern
p	purl
p-wise	purl wise
rem	remain(ing)
rep	repeat
sl	slip
sl st	slip stitch
st(s)	stitch(es)
st-st	stocking stitch (one row k, one row p)
tbl	through back of loop
tog	together
w(y) bk	wool (yarn) back
w(y) fwd	wool (yarn) forward
w(y) rn	wool (yarn) round needle
w(y) 2rn	wool (yarn) twice round needle
w(y) on	wool (yarn) on needle.

Crochet abbreviations

ch	chain
dc	double crochet
tr	treble
sl st	slip stitch

Detail of patchwork 'Fair Isle' design from Missoni of Italy

Casting on

Before you can knit a stitch, you have to cast it on. There are many ways of doing this and we give five methods here, each good for its purpose. Learn the thumb method first; the others can follow as you become more expert.

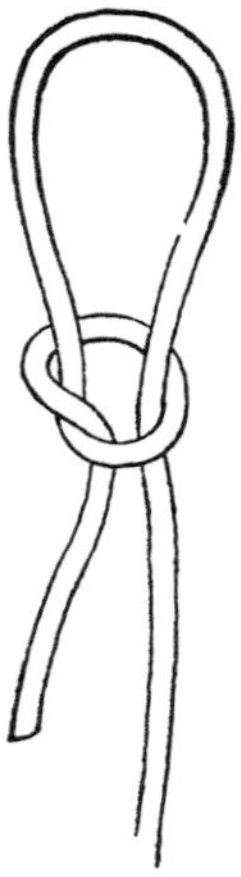

1

Slip loop

Thumb method of casting on

All knitting begins with a slip loop (fig. 1). Make a slip loop leaving an end of yarn sufficient for the number of stitches required (one yard is enough for 100 stitches on No 9 needles in 3 or 4-ply yarn), and place on needle, drawing up both ends of yarn to tighten the loop. Hold the needle in your right hand and the loose end of yarn in your left hand (fig. 2). * Wind the loose end of yarn round thumb of left hand, insert needle point through loop (fig. 3), wind main yarn round needle and draw loop through, (fig. 4). Leave stitch thus made on needle, and repeat from * for required number of stitches. For an extra strong edge, have the loose end of yarn double.

Cable method of casting on with two needles

Make a slip loop on the left-hand needle. Put right-hand needle into loop, yarn round the right-hand needle (fig. 5), draw through loop on left-hand needle and transfer loop to left-hand needle (fig. 6); * insert the right-hand needle between the last two stitches on the left-hand needle (fig. 7), yarn round right-hand needle, draw the loop through and transfer the stitch made on to the left-hand needle (fig. 8); repeat from * for the required number of stitches.

Looped method of casting on using one needle

This method is used when a very loose cast on edge is required, for instance, for lace patterns, scallops, button-holes or when hems are

knitted up. Make a slip loop on the right-hand needle, * loop yarn round left thumb and put loop on needle (fig. 9); repeat from * for the required number of stitches.

Cable method of casting on with four needles

Sets of four needles pointed at both ends are required for this method. With two needles, cast on the required number of stitches on one needle, by the cable method. Using the third needle, cast the required number of stitches on the next needle and using the fourth, cast the required number of stitches on the next needle. Make sure that the stitches are not twisted, and that the last stitch on the last needle is drawn up close to the first stitch on the first needle for the next row, thus forming a triangle. The right side of the work is always on the outside, facing you (fig. 10).

Circular method of casting on, worked on circular needle

Cast on the required number of stitches by the cable method, making sure that the last stitch on the needle is drawn up close to the first stitch to avoid a loose stitch. The right side of the work is always facing you.

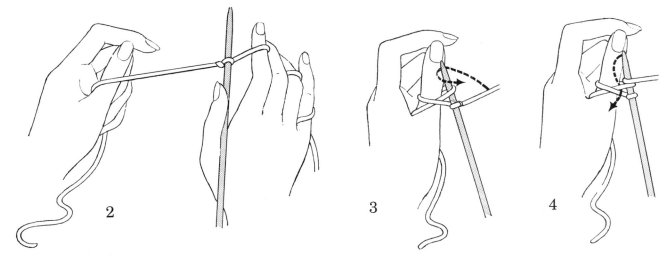

Thumb method

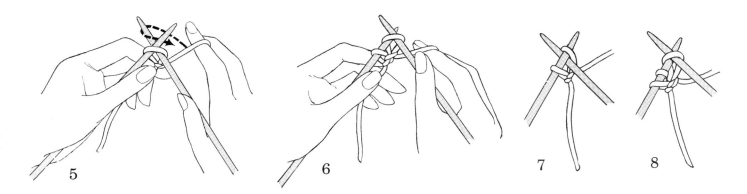

Cable method

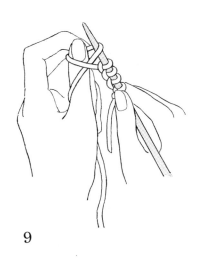

Looped method

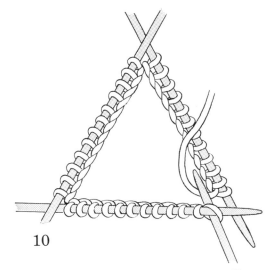

Cable method with four needles

9

Knitting and purling

Once you have cast on your stitches, you can begin to knit. It is preferable to use long firm needles, so that you can hold the right-hand needle under your right arm, thus leaving your right hand free to manipulate the yarn.

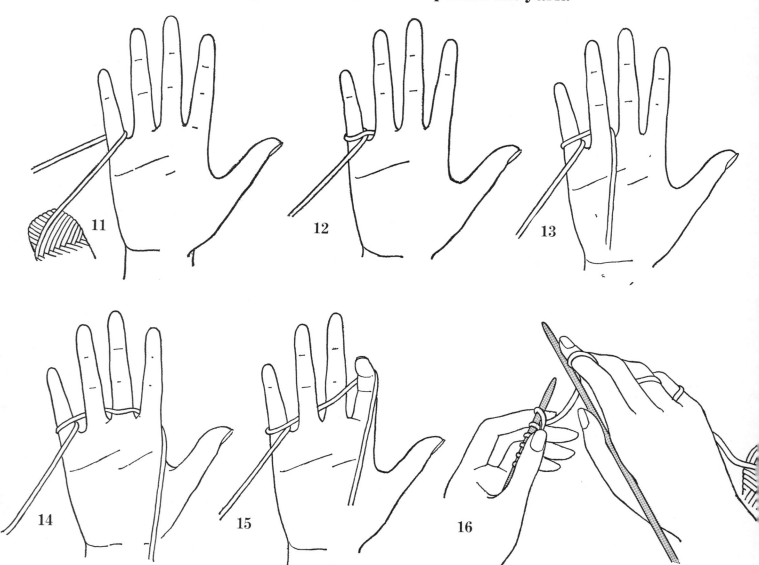

To achieve firm, even knitting

Loop yarn from palm of right hand between your fourth and third fingers (fig. 11), round the fourth finger and back between the fourth and third fingers (fig. 12), over the third finger, between the third and second fingers (fig. 13), under the second finger and over the index finger (fig. 14). Holding the yarn in this way (fig. 15), place the right-hand needle in the crook of your hand between thumb and palm; use only the index finger of this hand to manipulate the yarn, allowing the needle to slide between thumb and hand (fig. 16).

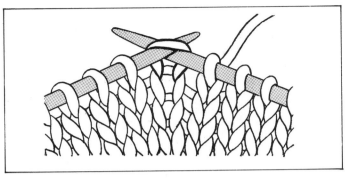

17

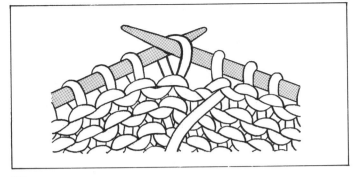

20

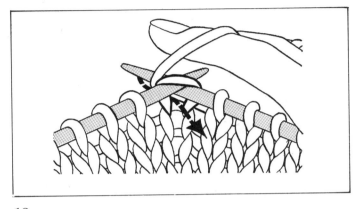

18

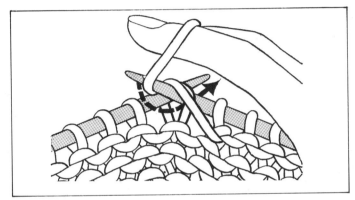

21

To knit

Hold the needle containing the cast on stitches in your left-hand; keeping yarn at back of work, * put right-hand needle through front of 1st stitch from left to right (fig. 17), with right-hand index finger put yarn round point of right-hand needle from below and between two needle points (fig. 18), turn needle point and hook loop just made through stitch on left-hand needle; keep the stitch just made on the right-hand needle and slip old stitch off left-hand needle. Repeat from * until all stitches have been knitted. The side of the work facing you is known as 'knit' or 'plain' fabric (fig. 19).

To purl

Hold the needle containing the cast on stitches in your left-hand, keeping yarn at front of work, * put right-hand needle through front of 1st stitch from right to left

(fig. 20), with right-hand index finger put yarn from above round point of right-hand needle (fig. 21), turn needle point and hook loop just made through stitch on left-hand needle; keep new stitch just made on right-hand needle and slip old stitch off left-hand needle; repeat from * until all stitches have been purled. The side of the work facing you is known as 'purl' fabric (fig. 22).

Knitting in style

As soon as you have learned to knit and purl, begin to develop your own knitting style. We have given a way of holding needles and yarn as a guide, but the important thing is to develop a style which you find easy and comfortable and that gives you complete control over the yarn as it forms a stitch; this is vital if you are to achieve regular and even tension.

19

22

Basic stitches

All hand-knitting patterns are based on variations in knitting and purling and once you have mastered these, making sure that the fabric is firm and even, you will be ready to go on to more complicated stitches. The following illustrations show variations in basic knitting and purling.

Garter-stitch (fig. 23)
This fabric is formed by knitting every row; the same effect can be achieved by purling every row.

Stocking-stitch (fig. 24)
This fabric is formed by knitting one row and purling one row, alternately. The knit side of the fabric forms 'stocking-stitch' and the purl side forms 'reversed stocking-stitch'.

Ribbing (fig. 25)
The closest form of ribbing is knit one, purl one rib. This is formed by * knitting one stitch, put the yarn forward between the needles and purl the next stitch, put the yarn back between the needles and repeat from * all along the row. On the next row all the knitted stitches will be purled and all the purled stitches will be knitted. There are many variations in ribbing but they are usually worked by knitting so many stitches, then purling so many stitches and working the following row in reverse.

Moss-stitch (fig. 26)
This fabric is worked by knitting one stitch and purling one stitch along the row, as in knit one purl one ribbing, but on the next row the knitted stitches are knitted and the purled stitches purled. This is worked on all following rows.

Twisted stitches (fig. 27)
Normally stitches are worked as described previously but in some patterns a 'twisted' stitch is required. In this case the right-hand needle is put into the back of the stitch instead of the front and then knitted or purled in the usual way. The abbreviation for this is 'tbl' — through the back of the loop.

Slipped stitches (fig. 28)
Stitches can be slipped from the left-hand to the right-hand needle without being worked. To slip a stitch 'knitwise', put the needle into the stitch as though to knit it and slip it off the left-hand needle on to the right-hand needle; to slip one 'purlwise', put the needle into the stitch as though to purl it and slip it from the left-hand needle to the right-hand needle. To form a neat edge on a garment, particularly on something like a border for a cardigan, slip the first stitch on *every* row knitwise and *knit* the last stitch in *every* row. This forms a small 'pip' and makes row counting easy, as one 'pip' equals two rows; it also helps when making up garments, to match up the sides for sewing.

12

23

24

25

26

27

28

13

Tension

You have now learned the basic steps in knitting but unless you read the following chapter — which is the most important of all in hand-knitting — very carefully, you will never achieve satisfactory results.

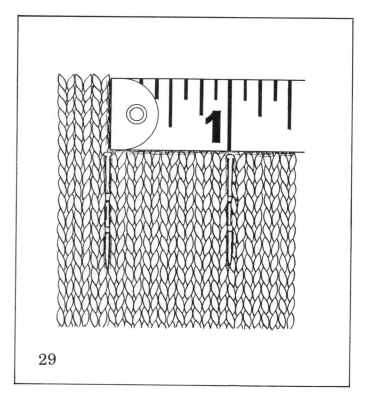

29

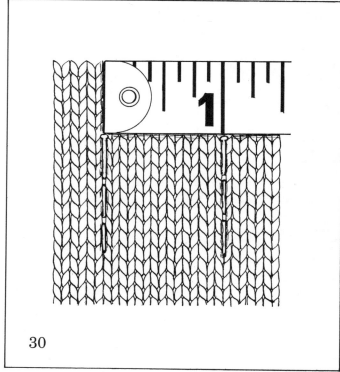

30

The word 'tension' simply means the number of stitches and rows in a given measurement, usually one inch, which has been achieved by the designer of the garment with the yarn and needle size stated. In any reliable knitting pattern, the tension has been checked many times by different knitters before the instructions are printed but although this most important point is stressed in every knitting leaflet and magazine published, it is all too often overlooked. Every knitter assumes that her tension is correct because she will knit in the way which comes easily and naturally to her but where the wording, 'check your tension' appears, it does not imply that your knitting will be inaccurate; it is merely to stress that this particular tension has been worked by the designer and unless you work to the same tension you will not obtain the same results. Using the correct yarn and needle size stated, if the tension is given as, say, 7 stitches to the inch, your fabric will be firm and even (fig. 29). If, instead of 7 stitches to the inch, your tension is 7½ stitches, your fabric will be too tight (fig. 30) and if your tension is 6¼ stitches to the inch, it will be too loose (fig. 31). Even a quarter of a stitch difference in tension can make an overall difference in measurements of two inches or more, so that if tension is incorrect a 32″ size sweater could become a 34″ or 30″ size.

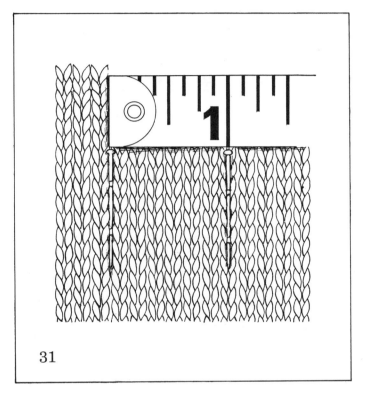

31

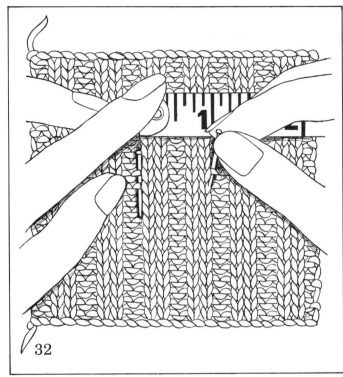

32

How to check your tension

Before commencing any garment, work a small stitch sample about four inches square in the main pattern and on the needles stated. Place the knitted sample on a flat surface and mark out one inch with pins (fig. 32). Count the number of stitches and rows very carefully and if your tension is correct then you can begin the design of your choice. If you have any doubt at all, mark out two, or even three inches with pins as a further check. Say the tension given is 7 stitches and 9 rows to one inch; then, having cast on 28 stitches and worked 36 rows you should have a sample measuring exactly 4 inches by 4 inches. If you have fewer stitches to the inch than stated, your tension is too loose and you should work another sample using a size smaller needle. If you have more stitches to the inch, then your tension is too tight and you should work another sample using a size larger needle. Continue in this way, altering the size of your needles, until you obtain the correct tension given; only then is it safe to start the pattern. Most instructions state the number of stitches in width and the number of rows in depth; if you have to choose between obtaining one but not the other, then the *width* tension is the most important, as length can be adjusted by working more or less rows as required. Do not read beyond this chapter until you are confident that you have understood the importance of tension in hand-knitting.

Shaping

All shaping is worked by adding to, or taking away from, the number of stitches on a row. Increasing a stitch means adding a stitch and decreasing a stitch means losing a stitch. Single stitches can be increased or decreased at either end of a row, or shaping can be worked in the centre of a row. Groups of stitches are increased or decreased by casting on or casting off. Stitches are usually only cast off for shaping at the beginning of a row; if they are cast off at the end of a row the yarn must be broken off and rejoined to work the next row. Shaping details are usually set out quite clearly in knitting instructions.

Decreasing

Casting off
This method is used where blocks of stitches are to be decreased, such as shoulder and neck shaping. Casting off should always be worked slightly looser than the rest of your work, particularly round neckbands, and you may find it easier to use a size larger needle.

Casting off on a knit row
Knit the first two stitches, * with the point of the left-hand needle lift the first stitch over the 2nd stitch and off the needle, leaving one stitch on the right-hand needle (fig. 33), knit the next stitch. Repeat from * until one stitch remains, break off yarn leaving a 6-inch end, draw yarn through stitch and pull tight. Or, cast off required number of stitches then knit to the end of the row (fig. 34).

Casting off on a purl row
Purl the first two stitches, * put yarn back between needles; with the point of left-hand needle lift first stitch over 2nd stitch and off the needle leaving one stitch on right-hand needle (fig. 35); put yarn forward between needles, purl the next stitch; repeat from * until one stitch remains, break off yarn leaving a 6-inch end, draw yarn through stitch and pull tight. Or, cast off required number of stitches then purl to end of row (fig. 36).

Casting off in pattern
Work each stitch in pattern before casting off as given above. Or, cast off required number of stitches, pattern to end of row, making sure to keep a sequence of pattern correct (fig. 37).

Casting off on four needles
Cast off stitches on first needle as given above, work first stitch on 2nd needle, with point of left-hand needle lift last stitch on first needle over first stitch on 2nd needle, work 1 stitch; continue casting off on 2nd needle and 3rd needle in same way until one stitch remains. Break off yarn, leaving a 6-inch end, draw yarn through stitch and pull tight (fig. 38).

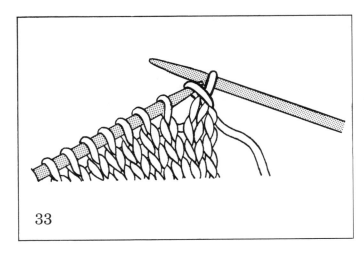

33

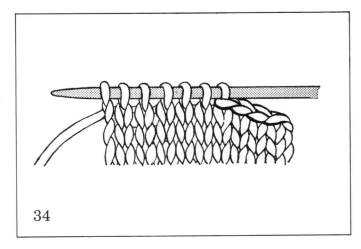

34

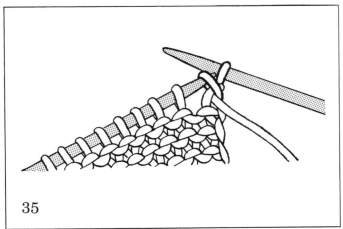

35

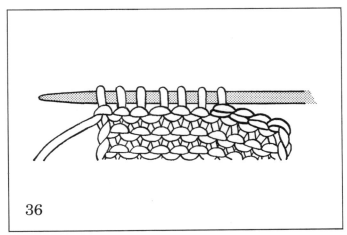

36

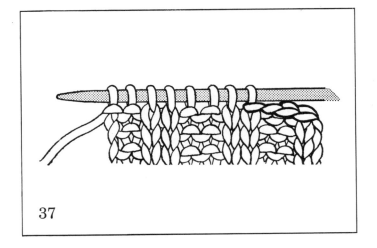

37

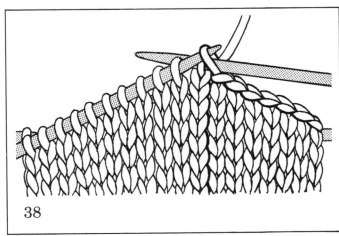

38

Shaping

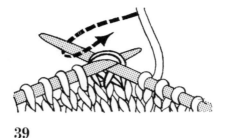

39

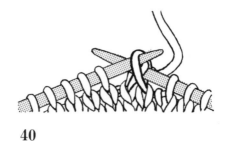

40

41

Decreasing on a knit row

1. To decrease one stitch, put right-hand needle *knitwise* through the next two stitches and knit them together in the usual way. The abbreviation for this is 'k 2 tog' and it makes a stitch leaning to the right (fig. 39).

2. To decrease one stitch, slip the next stitch *purlwise* on to the right-hand needle, knit the next stitch, put the point of the left-hand needle, purl-wise into the slipped-stitch and lift this over the knitted stitch, and off the right-hand needle. The abbreviation for this is 'sl 1, k 1, psso' and it makes a stitch leaning to the left (fig. 40).

3. To decrease two stitches, put the right-hand needle *knitwise* through the next three stitches and knit them together in the usual way. The abbreviation for this is 'k 3 tog' and it makes a stitch leaning to the right (fig. 41).

4. To decrease two stitches, slip next stitch *purlwise* on to the right-hand needle, knit the next two stitches together, put the point of the left-hand needle *purlwise* into the slipped stitch and lift this over the two stitches knitted together and off the right-hand needle.

The abbreviation for this 'sl 1, K2 tog, psso' and it makes a stitch leaning to the left (fig. 42).

Decreasing on a purl row

1. To decrease one stitch, put the right-hand needle purlwise through the next two stitches and purl them together in the usual way. The abbreviation for this is 'p 2 tog', it shows on the knit fabric as a stitch leaning to the right (fig. 43).

2. To decrease one stitch, put the right hand needle through the back of the next two stitches from left to right and purl them together in the usual way. The abbreviation for this is 'p 2 tog tbl' and it shows on the knit fabric as a stitch leaning to the left (fig. 44).

Shaping by decreasing

Shaping can be worked at the ends of rows by knitting or purling two together as given above or in the centre of a row as dart shaping. Fully-fashioned shapings are usually worked a few stitches in from the ends of the rows.

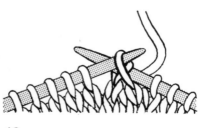

42

43

44

18

45

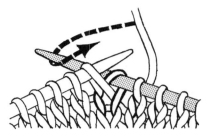

46

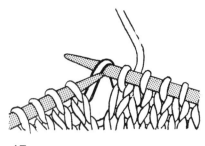

47

Increasing

Casting on

Cast on the required number of stitches at the beginning of a row by the cable method given on page 8 or, if given in the instructions, at the end of a row by the loop method given on page 8.

Increasing by means of a stitch

1. Increase one stitch on a knit row by knitting first into the front and then into the back of the same stitch before slipping stitch off left-hand needle, and on a purl row by purling into the front and back of the same stitch (fig. 45). The abbreviation for this is 'inc 1'. For special effects, which will be given in the instructions, you can also knit 1 then purl 1 into the same stitch, or purl 1 then knit 1.

2. Increase one stitch by putting the point of the right-hand needle into the stitch below the next stitch on the left-hand needle and knit this, then knit the stitch from the left-hand needle. The abbreviation for this is 'm 1', and this method can also be worked on a purl row (fig. 46).

3. Increase one stitch by picking up with the point of the right-hand needle the loop lying between the stitches on the left and right-hand needles, place loop on left-hand needle and knit or purl into the back of the loop. The abbreviation for this is 'k up l' and it makes an almost invisible increased stitch (fig. 47).

Increasing by means of a loop

This method is only used for special effects as it makes a hole; it is the basis of all lace patterns

1. To make a stitch by means of a loop on a knit row, bring the yarn forward between the needles then knit the next stitch in the usual way, carrying the yarn over the right-hand needle. The abbreviation for this is 'y fwd' (fig. 48).

2. To make a loop on a purl row take the yarn over and round right-hand needle to front, then purl next stitch in the usual way. The abbreviation for this is 'y rn' (fig. 49).

3. To make a loop between a purl and a knit stitch, purl stitch in the usual way then take yarn over right-hand needle and knit the next stitch in the usual way. The abbreviation for this is 'y on' (fig. 50).

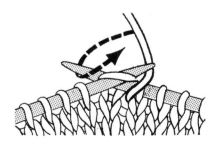

48

49

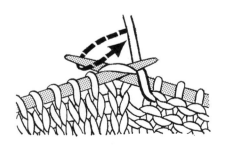

50

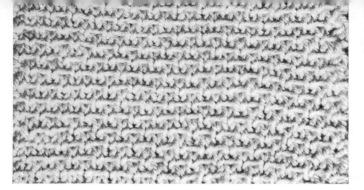

51

52

Patterned stitches

Provided you have mastered all the preceding stages and can knit in an even and relaxed way, you are now ready to begin more complicated stitches.

Use oddments of 4-ply yarn and a pair of No 10 needles; a cable needle should also be available in the same size.

The multiples of stitches given represent one complete pattern repeat and where, for example, four stitches are used, it would be advisable to cast on 20 stitches, plus any end stitches, making five complete pattern repeats. Work at least 3″ of each stitch to make sure you have understood the pattern.

You will notice that all the instructions are written in an abbreviated form and explana-tions for these terms are given on page 7, but there is one point which should be explained before you begin these samples. This is the practice of enclosing a set of stitches in square brackets [ ], followed by a figure. This is done to save space and means that the stitches given in the brackets must be repeated a certain number of times. For example in the Moss and Rib stitch (fig. 55) the first row states [p 1, k 1] 3 times; this means that you must p 1, k 1, p 1, k 1, p 1, k 1, before continuing with the pattern.

Fabric Stitch (fig. 51)

Cast on an even number of sts.
1st row: * K 1, y fwd, sl 1 purlwise, y bk; rep from * to end.
2nd row: P to end.
3rd row: * Y fwd, sl 1 purlwise, y bk, k 1; rep from * to end.

4th row: P to end.
These four rows form patt.

Fancy rib (fig. 52)
Cast on multiples of 4 sts plus 1.
1st row: Sl 1, * p 3, k 1; rep from * to end.
2nd row: Sl 1, * k 3, p 1; rep from * to last st, k 1.
These two rows form patt.

53

54

55

56

Fancy rib (fig. 53)

Cast on multiples of 4 sts plus 3.

1st row: Sl 1, k 1, * insert needle into next 3 sts purlwise, p 1, k 1, p 1 into these 3 sts – called PM3 – k 1; rep from * to last st, k 1.

2nd row: Sl 1, p to last st, k 1.

These two rows form patt.

Fancy rib (fig. 54)

Cast on odd number of stitches.

1st row: Sl 1, k to end.

2nd row: Sl 1, * p 1, k 1; rep from * to end of row.

These two rows form patt.

Moss and rib (fig. 55)

Cast on multiples of 12 plus 7.

1st row: [P 1, k 1] 3 times, * p 2, k 1, p 1, k 1, p 2, [k 1, p 1] twice, k 1; rep from * to last st, p 1.

2nd row and every alt row: K all k sts and p all p sts.

3rd row: P 1, * k 1, p 1; rep from * to end.

5th row: As 1st row.

7th row: [K 1, p 1] twice, k 1, * p 2, [k 1, p 1] twice, k 1, p 2, k 1, p 1, k 1; rep from * to last 2 sts, p 1, k 1.

9th row: As 3rd row.

11th row: As 7th row.

12th row: K all k sts and p all p sts.

Ladder lace rib (fig. 56)

Cast on multiples of 5 sts plus 2.

1st row: [Wrong side] K 2, * p 3 tog, k 2; rep from * to end.

2nd row: P 2, * y rn, p 1, y rn, p 2; rep from * to end.

These two rows form patt.

Sailor's rib (fig. 57)

Cast on multiples of 5 sts plus 1.

1st row: [Right side] K 1 tbl, p 1, k 2, p 1, k 1 tbl; rep from * to end.

2nd row: P 1, * k 1, p 2, k 1, p 1; rep from * to end.

3rd row: K 1 tbl, * p 4, k 1 tbl; rep from * to end.

4th row: P 1, * k 4, p 1; rep from * to end.

These four rows form patt.

Cable stitch (fig. 58)

Cast on multiples of 9 plus 5.

1st row: Sl 1, * p 3, k 6; rep from * to last 4 sts, p 3, k 1.

2nd row: Sl 1, * k 3, p 6; rep from * to last 4 sts, k 4.

Rep these two rows once more.

5th row: Sl 1, * p 3, sl next 3 sts on to a cable needle and hold at back of work, k 3 sts from left-hand needle, k 3 sts from cable needle – called C3B; rep from * to last 4 sts, p 3, k 1.

6th row: As 2nd.

Rep 1st and 2nd rows three times more.

13th row: Sl 1, * p 3, sl next 3 sts on to cable needle and hold at front of work, k 3 sts from left-hand needle, k 3 sts from cable needle – called C3F; rep from * to last 4 sts, p 3, k 1.

14th row: As 2nd.

Rep 1st and 2nd rows once more.

These 16 rows form patt.

57

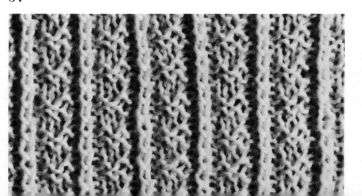

58

Patterned stitches

59

Rib and chevron (fig. 59)
Cast on multiples of 14 sts.

1st row: [Right side] * K 1, p 4, k 4, p 4, k 1; rep from * to end.

2nd row and every alt row: K all k sts and p all p sts.

3rd row: * K 1, p 3, k 6, p 3, k 1; rep from * to end.

5th row: * K 1, p 2, [k 2, p 1] twice, k 2, p 2, k 1; rep from * to end.

7th row: * K 1, p 1, [k 2, p 2] twice, k 2, p 1, k 1; rep from * to end.

9th row: * K 3, p 3, k 2, p 3, k 3; rep from * to end.

11th row: * K 2, [p 4, k 2] twice; rep from * to end.

13th row: K 1, * p 5, k 2; rep from * to last 6 sts, p 5, k 1.

14th row: As 2nd row.

These 14 rows form patt.

Gooseberry stitch (fig. 60)
Cast on an odd number of sts.

1st row: [Right side] K.

2nd row: K 1, * [p 1, y rn, p 1, y rn, p 1] into next st making 5 sts from one st, k 1; rep from * to end.

3rd row: P.

4th row: K 1, * sl 2 with yarn at front of work, p 3 tog, p2sso, k 1; rep from * to end.

5th row: K.

6th row: K 2, * [p 1, y rn, p 1, y rn, p 1] into next st, k 1; rep form * to last st, k 1.

7th row: P.

8th row: K 2, * sl 2 with yarn at front of work, p 3 tog, p2sso, k 1; rep from * to last st, k 1.

These eight rows form patt.

Cable and ladder stitch (fig. 61)
Cast on multiples of 14 sts plus 1.

1st row: [Wrong side] K 1, * p 2 tog, y rn, p 11, k 1; rep from * to end.

2nd row: K 1, * sl 1, k 1, psso, y fwd, sl next 3 sts on to cable needle and hold at back of work, k 3, k 3 from cable needle, k 6; rep from * to end.

3rd row: As 1st row.

4th row: K 1, * sl 1, k 1, psso, y fwd, k 12; rep from * to end.

5th row: As 1st row.

6th row: K 1, * sl 1, k 1, psso, y fwd, k 3, sl next 3 sts on to cable needle and hold at front of work, k 3, k 3 from cable needle, k 3; rep from * to end.

7th row: As 1st row.

8th row: As 4th row.

These eight rows form patt.

Anemone stitch (fig. 62)
Cast on multiples of 4 sts.

1st row: [Wrong side] P each st putting yarn twice round needle for each st.

2nd row: * Sl 4 sts on to right-hand needle dropping extra yarn and making 4 long sts, replace these sts on to left-hand needle, [k 4 tog, p 4 tog] twice into these sts; rep from * to end.

3rd row: P 2, p to last 2 sts putting yarn twice round needle for each st, p 2.

4th row: K 2, * sl 4 sts on to right hand needle dropping extra yarn and making 4 long sts, replace these sts on to left-hand needle, [k 4 tog, p 4 tog] twice into these

60

61

62

63

sts; rep from * to last 2 sts, k 2.
These four rows form patt.

Steep diagonal rib (fig. 63)
Cast on multiples of 6 sts.
1st row: * P 3, k 3; rep from * to end.
2nd row and every alt row: K all k sts and p all p sts.
3rd row: P 2, * k 3, p 3; rep from * to last 4 sts, k 3, p 1.
5th row: P1, * k 3, p 3; rep from * to last 5 sts, k 3, p 2.
7th row: * K 3, p 3; rep from * to end.
9th row: K 2, * p 3, k 3; rep from * to last 4 sts, p 3, k 1.
11th row: K 1, * p 3, k 3; rep from * to last 5 sts, p 3, k 2.
12th row: K all k sts and p all p sts.
These twelve rows form patt.

Fancy lozenge pattern (fig. 64)
Cast on multiples of 18 sts plus 2.
1st row: [Right side] P 2, * k 4, p 4, k 2, p 2, k 4, p 2; rep from * to end.
2nd row: K 3, * p 4, k 2, p 2, k 2, p 4, k 4; rep from * ending last rep k 3, instead of k 4.
3rd row: K 2, * p 2, k 4, p 4, k 4, p 2, k 2; rep from * to end.
4th row: P 1, * k 4, [p 4, k 2] twice, p 2; rep from * to last st, k 1.
5th row: P 2, * k 2, p 2, k 8, p 2, k 2, p 2; rep from * to end.
6th row: K 1, * p 2, k 4, p 6, k 2, p 2, k 2; rep from * to last st, p 1.
7th row: K 2, * p 2, k 2, p 2, k 4, [p 2, k 2] twice; rep from * to end.

8th row: P 1, * k 2, p 2, k 2, p 6, k 4, p 2; rep from * to last st, k 1.
9th row: As 5th row.
10th row: K 1, * p 2, [k 2, p 4] twice, k 4; rep from * to last st, p 1.
11th row: As 3rd row.
12th row: As 2nd row.
13th row: P 2, * k 4, p 2, k 2, p 4, k 4, p 2; rep from * to end.
14th row: P 5, * [k 2, p 2] twice, k 2, p 8; rep from * ending last rep p 5.
15th row: K 4, * [p 2, k 2] twice, p 4, k 6; rep from * ending last rep, k 4.
16th row: P 3, * [k 2, p 2] 3 times, k 2, p 4; rep from * ending last rep, p 3.
17th row: K 4, * p 4, [k 2, p 2] twice, k 6; rep from * ending last rep, k 4.
18th row: As 14th row.
These 18 rows form patt.

Braid stitch (fig. 65)
Cast on multiples of 8 sts plus 4.
1st row: [Wrong side] K 4, * p 4, k 4; rep from * to end.
2nd row: P 4, *[sl 1 with yarn at back of work, k 1, y rn, pass sl-st over k st and y rn st] twice, p 4; rep from * to end.
3rd row: As 1st.
4th row: P 4, * k 1, sl 1 with yarn at back of work, k 1, y rn, pass sl-st over k st and y rn st, k 1, p 4; rep from * to end.
These four rows form patt.

64

65

Lace stitches

You are now ready for more exciting knitting, but obviously these stitches are more difficult than those in the previous section, so take extra care. You will already have come across most of the abbreviations used, but some of them will be new to you so refer to the abbreviations listed on page 7.

You should try these stitches using No 10 needles and 4-ply yarn as you will find these intricate stitches easier to follow at first using a thicker yarn and larger needles; once you become more competent remember that they are really beautiful when knitted in fine yarn on small needles.

Harebell stitch (fig. 66)
Cast on multiples of 8 sts plus 3.
1st row: Sl 1, k 2 tog, * y fwd, k 1, y fwd, sl 1, k 2 tog psso; rep from * to last 4 sts, y fwd, k 1, y fwd, sl 1, k 1, psso, k 1.
2nd and every alt row: Sl 1, p to last st, k 1.
3rd row: Sl 1, k 2 tog, * y fwd, k 5, y fwd, sl 1, k 2 tog, psso; rep from * to last 8 sts, y fwd, k 5, y fwd, sl 1, k 1, psso, k 1.
5th row: As 3rd.
7th row: As 3rd.
9th row: Sl 1, k 2, * y fwd, sl 1, kl, psso, k 1, k 2 tog, y fwd, k 3; rep from * to end.
10th row: As 2nd.
These 10 rows form patt.

Spider stitch (fig. 67)
Cast on multiples of 6 sts plus 1.

1st row: [Wrong side] P.
2nd row: K 1, * y fwd, sl 1, k 1, psso, k 1, k 2 tog, y fwd, k 1; rep from * to end of row.
3rd row: P.
4th row: As 2nd.
5th row: As 1st.
6th row: As 2nd.
7th row: As 1st.
8th row: K 2, * y fwd, sl 1, k 2 tog, psso, y fwd, k 3; rep from * to end, ending last rep k 2 instead of k 3.
9th row: As 1st.
10th row: K 1, * k 2 tog, y fwd, k 1, y fwd, sl 1, k 1, psso, k 1; rep from * to end.
11th row: As 1st.
12th row: K 2 tog, * y fwd, k 3, y fwd, sl 1, k 2 tog, psso; rep from * to end ending last rep y fwd, k 3, y fwd, sl 1, k 1, psso.
These 12 rows form patt.

66

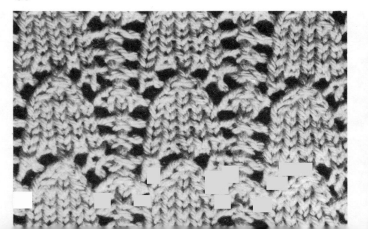

67

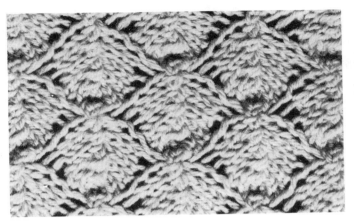

68

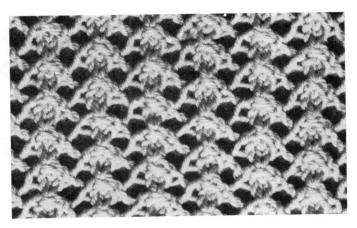

69

Shell pattern (fig. 68)

Cast on multiples of 10 plus 3.

1st row: Sl 1, * k 1, y fwd, k 2 tog tbl, k 5, k 2 tog, y fwd; rep from * to last 2 sts, k 2.

2nd and every alt row: Sl 1, p to last st, k 1.

3rd row: Sl 1, * k 1, y fwd, k 1, k 2 tog tbl, k 3, k 2 tog, k 1, y fwd; rep from * to last 2 sts, k 2.

5th row: Sl 1, * k 1, y fwd, k 2, k 2 tog.tbl, k 1, k 2 tog, k 2, y fwd; rep from * to last 2 sts, k 2.

7th row: Sl 1, * k 1, y fwd, k 3, k 3 tog, k 3, y fwd; rep from * to last 2 sts, k 2.

9th row: Sl 1, * k 3, k 2 tog, y fwd, k 1, y fwd, k 2 tog tbl, k 2; rep from * to last 2 sts, k 2.

11th row: Sl 1, * k 2, k 2 tog, [k 1, y fwd] twice, k 1, k 2 tog tbl, k 1; rep from * to last 2 sts, k 2.

13th row: Sl 1, * k 1, k 2 tog, k 2, y fwd, k 1, y fwd, k 2, k 2 tog tbl; rep from * to last 2 sts, k 2.

15th row: Sl 1, k 2 tog, * k 3, y fwd, k 1, y fwd, k 3, k 3 tog; rep from * to last 10 sts, k 3, y fwd, k 1, y fwd, k 3, k 2 tog tbl, k 1.

16th row: As 2nd.

These 16 rows form patt.

Simple lace pattern (fig. 69)

Cast on multiples of 6 plus 2.

1st row: Sl 1, * k 3, y fwd, sl 1, k 2 tog, psso, y fwd; rep

from * to last st, k 1.

2nd row: Sl 1, p to last st, k 1.

3rd row: Sl 1, * y fwd, sl 1, k 2 tog, psso, y fwd, k 3; rep from * to last st, k 1.

4th row: As 2nd;

These four rows form patt.

Lace rib pattern (fig. 70)

Cast on multiples of 4 plus 2.

1st row: Sl 1, * k 2, y fwd, sl 1, k 1, psso; rep from * to last st, k 1.

2nd row: Sl 1, * p 2, y rn, p 2 tog; rep from * to last st, k. 1.

These two rows form patt.

Open mock cable pattern (fig. 71)

Cast on multiples of 4 plus 2.

1st row: Sl 1, p 1, * k 1, y fwd, k 1, p 2; rep from * to last 4 sts, k 1, y fwd, k 1, p 1, k 1.

2nd row: Sl 1, k 1, * p 3, k 2,; rep from * to end of row.

3rd row: Sl 1, p 1, * y bk, sl 1, k 2, pass slipped stitch over k 2, p 2, rep from * to last 5 sts, y bk, sl 1, k 2, pass slipped st over k 2, p 1, k 1.

4th row: Sl 1, k 1, * p 2, k 2; rep from * to end of row.

These four rows form patt.

70

71

72

73

Lace stitches

Rosebud mesh (fig. 72)
Cast on multiples of 10 sts plus 1.
1st row: [Wrong side] P.
2nd row: K 2 tog, * y fwd, k 3, y fwd, k into front and back of next st, y fwd, k 3, y fwd, sl 1, k 2 tog, psso; rep from * ending last rep sl 1, k 1, psso, instead of sl 1, k 2 tog, psso.
3rd and every alt row: P.
4th row: Sl 1, k 1, psso, * y fwd, sl 2, k 1, p2sso, y fwd, k 2 tog, y fwd, sl 1, k 1, psso, [y fwd, sl 2, k 1, p2sso] twice; rep from * ending last rep k 2 tog instead of the 2nd sl 2, k 1, p2sso worked.
6th row: K 2, * k 2 tog, y fwd, k 3, y fwd, sl 1, k 1, psso, k 3; rep from * ending last rep k 2 instead of k 3.
8th row: K 1, * k 2 tog, y fwd, k 1 tbl, y fwd, sl 1, k 2 tog, psso, y fwd, k 1 tbl, y fwd, sl 1, k 1, psso, k 1; rep from * to end.
These eight rows form patt.

Pine pattern (fig. 73)
Cast on multiples of 12 sts plus 3.
1st row: Sl 1, k 2 tog, * k 4, y fwd, k 1, y fwd, k 4, k 3 tog; rep from * to last 12 sts, k 4, y fwd, k 1, y fwd, k 4, k 2 tog, k 1.
2nd row: Sl 1, p 2 tog, * [p 3, y rn] twice, p 3, p 3 tog; rep from * to last 12 sts, [p 3, y rn] twice, p 3, p 2 tog, k 1.
3rd row: Sl 1, k 2 tog, * k 2, y fwd, k 5, y fwd, k 2, k 3 tog; rep from * to last 12 sts, k 2, y fwd, k 5, y fwd, k 2

74

k 2 tog, k 1.
4th row: Sl 1, p 2 tog, * p 1, y rn, p 7, y rn, p 1, p 3 tog; rep from * to last 12 sts, p 1, y rn, p 7, y rn, p 1, p 2 tog, k 1.
5th row: Sl 1, k 2 tog, * y fwd, k 9, y fwd, k 3 tog; rep from * to last 12 sts, y fwd, k 9, y fwd, k 2 tog, k 1.
6th row: Sl 1, p 1, * y rn, p 4, p 3 tog, p 4, y rn, p 1; rep from * to last 13 sts, y rn, p 4, p 3 tog, p 4, y rn, p 1, k 1.
7th row: Sl 1, k 2, * y fwd, k 3, k 3 tog, k 3, y fwd, k 3; rep from * to end.
8th row: Sl 1, p 3, * y rn, p 2, p 3 tog, p 2, y rn, p 5; rep from * to last 11 sts, y rn, p 2, p 3 tog, p 2, y rn, p 3, k 1.
9th row: Sl 1, k 4 * y fwd, k 1, k 3 tog, k 1, y fwd, k 7; rep from * to last 10 sts, y fwd, k 1, k 3 tog, k 1. y fwd, k 5.
10th row: Sl 1, p 5, * y rn, p 3 tog, y rn, p 9; rep from * to last 9 sts, y rn, p 3 tog, y rn, p 5, k 1.
These 10 rows form patt.

Lacy Chevron (fig. 74)
Cast on multiples of 8 sts plus 1.
1st row: [Right side] K 1, * sl 1, k 1, psso, [k 1, y fwd] twice, k 1, k 2 tog, k 1; rep from * to end.
2nd row: P 1, * p 2 tog, [p 1, y rn] twice, p 1, p 2 tog tbl, p 1; rep from * to end.
3rd row: K 1, * y fwd, sl 1, k 1, psso, k 3, k 2 tog, y fwd, k 1; rep from * to end.
4th row: P 2, * y rn, p 2 tog, p 1, p 2 tog tbl, y rn, p 3; rep from * ending last rep p 2 instead of p 3.
5th row: K 3, * y fwd, sl 2, k 1, p2sso, y fwd, k 5; rep from * ending last rep k 3 instead of k 5.
6th row: As 2nd row.
7th row: As 1st row.
8th row: P 1, * y rn, p 2 tog, p 3, p 2 tog tbl, y rn, p 1; rep from * to end of row.
9th row: K 2, * y fwd, sl 1, k 1, psso, k 1, k 2 tog, y fwd, k 3; rep from * ending last rep k 2 instead of k 3.
10th row: P 3, * y rn, sl 2, p 1, p2sso, y rn, p 5; rep from * ending last rep p 3 instead of p 5.
These 10 rows form patt.

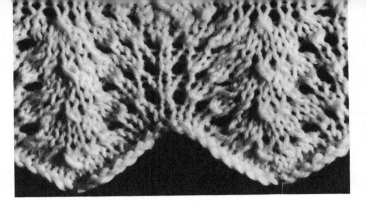

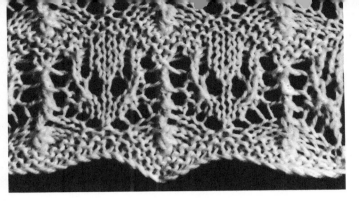

75

76

Ostrich plumes (fig. 75)

Cast on multiples of 16 sts plus 1.

1st row: [Wrong side and every wrong side row] P.

2nd row: K.

4th row: [K 1, y fwd] 3 times, * [sl 1, k 1, psso] twice, sl 2 k-wise, k 1, p2sso, [k 2 tog] twice, [y fwd, k 1] 5 times, y fwd; rep from * ending last rep [y fwd, k 1] 3 times instead of [y fwd, k 1] 5 times, y fwd.

6th row: As 2nd.

8th row: As 4th.

10th row: As 2nd.

12th row: As 4th.

14th row: As 2nd.

16th row: As 4th.

18th row: As 2nd.

20th row: [K 2 tog] 3 times, * [y fwd, k 1] 5 times, y fwd, [sl 1, k 1, psso] twice, sl 2 k-wise, k 1, p2sso [k 2 tog] twice; rep from * ending last rep [y fwd k 1] 5 times, y fwd, [sl 1, k 1, psso] 3 times.

22nd row: As 2nd.

24th row: As 20th.

26th row: As 2nd.

28th row: As 20th

30th row: As 2nd.

32nd row: As 20th.

These 32 rows form patt.

Lotus pattern (fig. 76)

Cast on multiples of 10 sts plus 1.

1st–5th row: K.

6th row: [Wrong side] P 1, * y rn, p 3, sl 2, p 1, p2sso, p 3, y rn, p 1; rep from * to end.

7th row: K 2, * y fwd, k 2, sl 2, k 1, p2sso, k 2, y rn, k 3; rep from * ending last rep k 2 instead of k 3.

8th row: P 3, * y rn, p 1, sl 2, p 1, p2sso, p 1, y rn, p 5; rep from * ending last rep p 3 instead of p 5.

9th row: K 4, * y fwd, sl 2, k 1, p2sso, y fwd, k 7; rep from * ending last rep k 4 instead of k 7.

10th row: P 2, * k 2, p 3; rep from * ending last rep p 2, instead of p 3.

11th row: K 1, * y rn, sl 1, k 1, psso, p 1, y rn, sl 2, k 1, p2sso, y rn, p 1, k 2 tog, y fwd, k 1; rep from * to end.

12th row: P 3, * k 1, p 3, k 1, p 5; rep from * ending last rep p 3 instead of p 5.

13th row: K 2, * y fwd, sl 1, k 1, psso, y fwd, sl 2, k 1, p2sso, y fwd, k 2 tog, y fwd, k 3; rep from * ending last rep k 2 instead of k 3.

14th row: P 2, * k 1, p 5, k 1, p 3; rep from * ending last rep p 2 instead of p 3.

15th row: K 2, * p 1, k 1, y fwd, sl 2, k 1, p2sso, y fwd, k 1, p 1, k 3; rep from * ending last rep k 2 instead of k 3.

16th row: As 14th.

These 16 rows form patt.

Lace puff (fig. 77)

Cast on multiples of 12 sts plus 2.

1st row: [Right side] K 1, * sl 1, k 1, psso, k 3, y rn, p 2, y fwd, k 3, k 2 tog; rep from * to last st, k 1.

2nd row: K 1, * p 2 tog, p 2, y fwd, k 4, y rn, p 2, p 2 tog tbl; rep from * to last st, k 1.

3rd row: K 1, * sl 1, k 1, psso, k 1, y rn, p 6, y fwd, k 1, k 2 tog; rep from * to last st, k 1.

4th row: K 1, * p 2 tog, y fwd, k 8, y rn, p 2 tog tbl; rep from * to last st, k 1.

5th row: K 1, * p 1, y fwd, k 3, k 2 tog, sl 1, k 1, psso, k 3, y rn, p 1; rep from * to last st, k 1.

6th row: K 1, * k 2, y rn, p 2, p 2 tog tbl, p 2 tog, p 2, y fwd, k 2; rep from * to last st, k 1.

7th row: K 1, * p 3, y fwd, k 1, k 2 tog, sl 1, k 1, psso, k 1, y rn, p 3; rep from * to last st, k 1.

8th row: K 1, * k 4, y rn, p 2 tog tbl, p 2 tog, y fwd, k 4; rep from * to last st, k 1.

These eight rows form patt.

77

Aran stitches

Traditional Aran stitches originated on the west coast of Ireland amongst the fishing families there. Each family had its own design and each man his own pattern. It was considered a matter of pride that a family should be known by its own variations on the traditional stitches. Many have religious associations as well as being taken from the day-to-day life of the fishermen. They have been handed down from generation to generation over the centuries and remain virtually unchanged today.

All Aran abbreviations will be given in the patterns but we give below the abbreviations used in the first two stitch patterns.

B1   Bobble 1. This is made by p 1, k 1, p 1 into the next st making 3 sts out of 1, turn and k these 3 sts, turn and p these 3 sts then sl the 2nd and 3rd st over the 1st st.

C1BB   Cross 1 and Bobble 1. Sl the next st on to cable needle and hold at back of work, k 1, Bl, k 1 from left-hand needle, p 1 from cable needle.

C3FB   Cross 3 and Bobble 1. Sl next 3 sts on to cable needle and hold at front of work, p 1 from left-hand needle, then k 1, Bl, k 1 on 3 sts on cable needle.

C1B   Cross 1 to back. Sl next st on cable needle and hold at back of work, k 3 from left-hand needle, k 1 tbl from cable needle.

C3F   Cross 3 front. Sl next 3 sts on to cable needle and hold at front of work, k 1 tbl from left-hand needle, k 3 from cable needle.

T2F   Twist 2 front. K into front of 2nd st on left-hand needle then into front of 1st st and sl off needle tog.

T2B   Twist 2 back. K into back of 2nd st on left-hand needle then into back of 1st st and sl off needle tog.

C2F   Cross 2 front. Sl next 2 sts on to cable needle and hold at front of work, k 3 from left-hand needle, then k 2 from cable needle.

C1BP   Cross 1 back and purl. Sl next st on to cable needle and hold at back of work, k 2 from left-hand needle, p 1 from cable needle.

C2FP   Cross 2 front and purl. Sl next 2 sts on to cable needle and leave at front of work, p 1 from left-hand needle, k 2 from cable needle.

C1KB   Cross 1 back and knit tbl. Sl next st on to cable needle and hold at back of work, k 2 from left-hand needle, k 1 tbl from cable needle.

C2FK   Cross 2 front and k. Sl next 2 sts on to cable needle and hold at front of work, k 1 from left-hand needle, k 2 from cable needle.

C1BK   Cross 1 back and k. Sl next st on to cable needle and hold at back of work, k 2 from left-hand needle, k 1 from cable needle.

M-st   Moss-st. Either k 1, p 1 or p 1, k 1, noting that on every following row k sts are knitted and p sts purled.

Aran pattern (1) (fig. 78)

Cast on multiples of 23 plus 2.

1st row: Sl 1, * p 8, k 3, k 1 tbl, k 3, p 8; rep from * to last st, k 1.

2nd row: Sl 1, * k 8, p 3, p 1 tbl, p 3, k 8; rep from * to last st, k 1.

3rd row: Sl 1, * p 7, C1BB, k 1 tbl, C3FB, p 7; rep from * to last st, k 1.

4th row: Sl 1, * k 7, p 3, k 1, p 1 tbl, k 1, p 3, k 7; rep from * to last st, k 1.

5th row: Sl 1, * p 6, C1B, p 1, k 1 tbl, p 1, C3F, p 6; rep from * to last st, k 1.

6th row: Sl 1, * k 6, p 3, [p 1 tbl, k 1] twice, p 1 tbl, p 3, k 6; rep from * to last st, k 1.

7th row: Sl 1, * p 5, C1BB, [k 1 tbl, p 1] twice, k 1 tbl, C3FB, p 5; rep from * to last st, k 1.

8th row: Sl 1, * k 5, p 3, [k 1, p 1 tbl] 3 times, k 1, p 3, k 5; rep from * to last st, k 1.

9th row: Sl 1, * p 4, C1B, [p 1, k 1 tbl] 3 times, p 1, C3F, p 4; rep from * to last st, k 1.

10th row: Sl 1, * k 4, p 3, [p 1 tbl, k 1] 4 times, p 1 tbl, p 3, k 4; rep from * to last st, k 1.

11th row: Sl 1, * p 3, C1BB, [k 1 tbl, p 1] 4 times, k 1 tbl, C3FB, p 3; rep from * to last st, k 1.

12th row: Sl 1, * k 3, p 3, [k 1, p 1 tbl] 5 times, k 1, p 3, k 3; rep from * to last st, k 1.

13th row: Sl 1, * p 2, C1B, [p 1, k 1 tbl] 5 times, p 1, C3F, p 2; rep from * to last st, k 1.

14th row: Sl 1, * k 2, p 3, [p 1 tbl, p 1] 6 times, p 1 tbl, p 3, k 2; rep from * to last st, k 1.

15th row: Sl 1, * p 1, C1BB, [k 1 tbl, p 1] 6 times, k 1 tbl, C3FB, p 1; rep from * to last st, k 1.

16th row: Sl 1, * k 1, p 3, [k 1, p 1 tbl] 7 times, k 1, p 3, k 1; rep from * to last st, k 1.

These 16 rows form patt.

Aran pattern (2) (fig. 79)

Cast on multiples of 31 sts plus 2.

1st row: Sl 1, * p 1, T2F, T2B, p 1, beg with k 1 m-st 6, k 7, beg with p 1 m-st 6, p 1, T2F, T2B, p 1; rep from * to last st, k 1.

2nd, 4th, 6th, 8th, 10th and 12th rows: Sl 1, * k 1, p 4, k 1, beg with k 1 m-st 6, k 1, p 5, k 1, beg with p 1 m-st 6, k 1, p 4, k 1; rep from * to last st, k 1.

3rd row: Sl 1, * p 1, T2B, T2F, p 1, m-st 6, k 1, C2F, k 1, m-st 6, p 1, T2B, T2F, p 1; rep from * to last st, k 1.

5th row: As 1st.

7th row: Sl 1, * p 1, T2B, T2F, p 1, m-st 6, k 7, m-st 6, p 1, T2B, T2F, p 1; rep from * to last st, k 1.

9th row: Sl 1, * p 1, T2F, T2B, p 1, m-st 6, k 1, C2F, k 1, m-st 6, p 1, T2F, T2B, p 1; rep from * to last st, k 1.

11th row: Sl 1, * p 1, T2B, T2F, p 1, m-st 6, k 7, m-st 6,

78

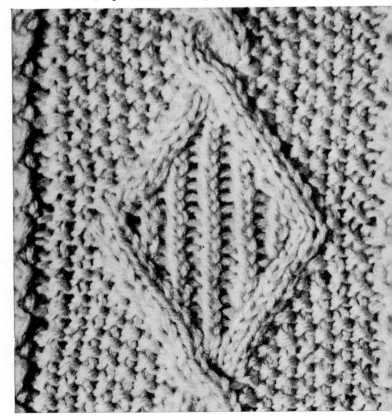

79

29

Aran stitches

80

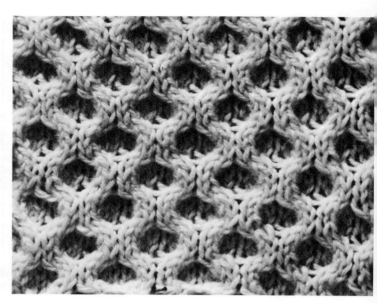

81

p 1, T2B, T2F, p 1; rep from * to last st, k 1.

13th row: Sl 1, * p 1, T2F, T2B, p 1, m-st 6, C1BP, k 1 tbl, C1FP, m-st 6, p 1, T2F, T2B, p 1; rep from * to last st, k 1.

14th row: Sl 1, * k 1, p 4, k 1, m-st 6, p 2, k 1, p 1 tbl, k 1, p 2, m-st 6, k 1, p 4, k 1; rep from * to last st, k 1.

15th row: Sl 1, * p 1, T2B, T2F, p 1, m-st 5, C1KB, p 1, k 1 tbl, p 1, C2FP, m-st 5, p 1, T2B, T2F, p 1; rep from * to last st, k 1.

16th row: Sl 1, * k 1, p 4, k 1, m-st 5, p 2, [p 1 tbl, k 1] twice, p 1 tbl, p 2, m-st 5, k 1, p 4, k 1; rep from * to last st, k 1.

17th row: Sl 1, * p 1, T2F, T2B, p 1, m-st 4, C1BP, [k 1 tbl, p 1] twice, k 1 tbl, C2FP, m-st 4, p 1, T2F, T2B, p 1; rep from * to last st, k 1.

18th row: Sl 1, * k 1, p 4, k 1, m-st 4, p 2, [k 1, p 1 tbl] 3 times, k 1, p 2, m-st 4, k 1, p 4, k 1; rep from * to last st, k 1.

19th row: Sl 1, * p 1, T2B, T2F, p 1, m-st 3, C1KB, [p 1, k 1 tbl] 3 times, p 1, C2FB, m-st 3, p 1, T2B, T2F, p 1; rep from * to last st, k 1.

20th row: Sl 1, * k 1, p 4, k 1, m-st 3, p 2, [p 1 tbl, k 1] 4 times, p 1 tbl, p 2, m-st 3, k 1, p 4, k 1; rep from * to last st, k 1.

21st row: Sl 1, * p 1, T2F, T2B, p 1, m-st 2, C1BP, [k 1 tbl, p 1] 4 times, k 1 tbl, C2FP, m-st 2, p 1, T2F, T2B, p 1; rep from * to last st, k 1.

22nd row: Sl 1, * k 1, p 4, k 1, m-st 2, p 2, [k 1, p 1 tbl] 5 times, k 1, p 2, m-st 2, k 1, p 4, k 1; rep from * to last st, k 1.

23rd row: Sl 1, * p 1, T2B, T2F, p 1, m-st 2, C2FK, [k 1 tbl, p 1] 4 times, k 1 tbl. C1BK, m-st 2, p 1, T2B,

T2F, p 1; rep from * to last st, k 1.

24th row: As 20th

25th row: Sl 1, * p 1, T2F, T2B, p 1, m-st 3, C2FP, [p 1, k 1 tbl] 3 times, p 1, C1BP, m-st 3, p 1, T2F, T2B, p 1; rep from * to last st, k 1.

26th row: As 18th

27th row: Sl 1, * p 1, T2B, T2F, p 1, m-st 4, C2FK, [k 1 tbl, p 1] twice, k 1 tbl, C1BK, m-st 4, p 1, T2B, T2F, p 1; rep from * to last st, k 1.

28th row: As 16th

29th row: Sl 1, * p 1, T2F, T2B, p 1, m-st 5, C2FP, p 1, k 1 tbl, p 1, C1BP, m-st 5, p 1, T2F, T2B, p 1; rep from * to last st, k 1.

30th row: As 14th.

31st row: Sl 1, * p 1, T2B, T2F, p 1, m-st 6, C2FK, k 1 tbl, C1BK, m-st 6, p 1, T2B, T2F, p 1; rep from * to last st, k 1.

32nd row: Sl 1, * k 1, p 4, k 1, m-st 7, p 2, p 1 tbl, p 2, m-st 7, k 1, p 4, k 1; rep from * to last st, k 1.
These 32 rows form patt.

Basket stitch (fig. 80)
Cast on multiples of 6 sts.

1st row: K.

2nd row: P.

3rd row: * Sl next 3 sts on to cable needle and hold at back of work, k next 3 sts, k 3 sts from cable needle — called C6B; rep from * to end.

4th row: P.

5th row: K.

6th row: P.

7th row: K 3, * sl next 3 sts on to cable needle and hold

82

83

at front of work, k next 3 sts, k 3 sts from cable needle — called C6F; rep from * to last 3 sts, k 3.
8th row: P.
These eight rows form patt.

Honeycomb stitch (fig. 81)

Cast on multiples of 8 sts plus 2.
1st row: K 1, * sl next 2 sts on to cable needle and hold at back of work, k next 2 sts, k 2 sts from cable needle — called C4B; sl next 2 sts on to cable needle and hold at front of work, k next 2 sts, k 2 sts from cable needle — called C4F; rep from * to last st, k 1.
2nd row: P.
3rd row: K.
4th row: P.
5th row: K 1, * C4F, C4B; rep from * to last st, k 1.
6th row: P.
7th row: K.
8th row: P.
These eight rows form patt.

Lobster claw (fig. 82)

Cast on multiples of 9 sts plus 2.
1st row: P 2, * k 7, p 2; rep from * to end.
2nd row: K 2, * p 7, k 2; rep from * to end.
3rd row: P 2, * sl next 2 sts on to cable needle and hold at back of work, k next st, k sts from cable needle, k 1, sl next st on to cable needle and hold at front of work, k next 2 sts, k st from cable needle, p 2; rep from * to end.
4th row: As 2nd.
These four rows form patt.

Tree of life (fig. 83)

Cast on multiples of 17 sts plus 2.
1st row: P 2, * p 6, k 3 tbl, p 8; rep from * to end.
2nd row: K 2, * k 6, p 3 tbl, k 8; rep from * to end.
3rd row: P 2, * p 5, sl next 2 sts on to cable needle and leave at back of work, k next st tbl, p st from cable needle — called T2F — k 1 tbl, sl next st on to cable needle and hold at front of work, p next st, k st from cable needle tbl — called T2B, p 7; rep from * to end.
4th row: K 2, * k 5, p 1 tbl, k 1, p 1 tbl, k 1, p 1 tbl, k 7; rep from * to end.
5th row: P 2, * p 4, T2F, p 1, k 1 tbl, p 1, T2B, p 6; rep from * to end.
6th row: K 2, * k 4, p 1 tbl, k 2, p 1 tbl, k 2, p 1 tbl, k 6; rep from * to end.
7th row: P 2, * p 3, T2F, p 2, k 1 tbl, p 2, T2B, p 5; rep from * to end.
8th row: K 2, * k 3, p 1 tbl, k 3, p 1 tbl, k 3, p 1 tbl, k 5; rep from * to end.
9th row: P 2, * p 2, T2F, p 3, k 1 tbl, p 3, T2B, p 4; rep from * to end.
10th row: K 2, * k 2, p 1 tbl, k 4, p 1 tbl, k 4, p 1 tbl, k 4; rep from * to end.
11th row: P 2, * p 1, T2F, p 4, k 1 tbl, p 4, T2B, p 3; rep from * to end.
12th row: K 2, * k 1, p 1 tbl, k 5, p 1 tbl, k 5, p 1 tbl, k 3; rep from * to end.
13th row: P 2, * T2F, p 5, k 1 tbl, p 5, T2B, p 2; rep from * to end.
14th row: K2, * p 1 tbl, k 6, p 1 tbl, k 6, p 1 tbl, k 2; rep from * to end.
These 14 rows form patt.

Fair Isle and tubular knitting

84

85

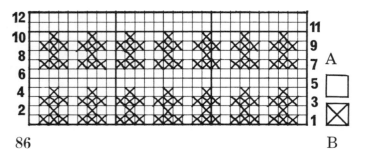

86

Two-colour knitting (fig. 84)

If a large number of stitches are to be worked in different colours, either vertically or in solid shapes in the garment, use a separate ball of yarn for each colour and twist the yarn firmly on the wrong side of the work when changing colours, to avoid making a hole.

Fair Isle or Norwegian knitting

These patterns are always worked in stocking-stitch, with groups of stitches knitted in different colours to form a pattern. The Fair Isle design is usually given in instructions as a chart, with each square representing one stitch and, unless illustrated in colour, a different symbol representing each colour. To work from a chart the odd numbered rows are the knit rows, the right side of the work, and the chart is read from RIGHT to LEFT. The purl rows are the even numbered rows, the wrong side of the work, and the chart is read from LEFT to RIGHT. See the illustration and chart of the simple Fair Isle pattern worked in two colours (figs. 85 and 86).

If you are working Fair Isle on four needles, or a circular needle, then every row on your chart will be a knit row and each row will read from Right to Left. There are two ways of working horizontal changes of colour in Fair Isle, either by stranding or by weaving the colour not in use across the back of the work.

Stranding method

When working the required number of stitches in one colour, the colour not in use is carried loosely at the back of the work until it is required. The colour in use is then dropped and the colour not in use taken up and used again, carrying the first colour loosely across the back of the work (fig. 87). The stranding method used over large pattern repeats can produce long strands at the back of the work between the changes of colour; since these strands easily catch and can distort the pattern, apart from causing annoyance to the wearer, it is better to combine both the stranding and weaving method for lengths of more than two or three stitches in each colour.

Weaving method

The colour in use is first taken *over* and then *under* the colour not in use on the wrong side of the work, thus:

With A only k one st, put B *over* right-hand needle at back of work and k next st with A only in usual way, k next st with A only holding B across back of work (fig. 88).

Fair Isle pattern in two colours (fig. 85)

With main shade, A cast on 29 sts.

1st row: [Right side] Working from chart from RIGHT to LEFT, * k 1 A, k 3 B; rep from * to last st, k 1 A.

2nd row: [Wrong side] Working from chart from LEFT to RIGHT, p 2 A, * p 1 B, p 3 A; rep from * to last 3 sts, p 1 B, p 2 A.

Continue working in this way from chart for the required number of rows (fig. 86).

Fair Isle pattern in three colours

With main shade, A, cast on multiples of 10 sts. Work from chart as given above from RIGHT to LEFT.

1st row: [Right side] * K 1 B, k 3 A, k 3 B, k 3 A; rep from * to end of row.

Continue working in this way from chart for the required number of rows, bringing in contrast colour C when indicated (fig. 89).

Tubular knitting

This makes a flat double fabric and is used for scarves, hems or piping (fig. 90).

Cast on an even number of sts.

1st row: * Yarn to front of work, sl 1 p-wise, yarn to back of work, k 1; rep from * to end of row. This row repeated gives a flat tube, with the knit fabric as the right side.

Double fabric can also be knitted in this way on four needles but an odd number of stitches must be cast on.

Two-colour tubular knitting

This is worked with a separate ball of each colour yarn and a pair of knitting needles pointed at both ends (fig. 91).

Cast on an even number of sts with main colour, A.

1st row: [Right side] With contrast colour, B, * k 1, y fwd, sl 1 p-wise, y bk; rep from * to end of row. DO NOT TURN WORK.

2nd row: [Right side again] With main shade, A, * sl 1 p-wise, y fwd, p 1, y bk; rep from * to end of row. TURN

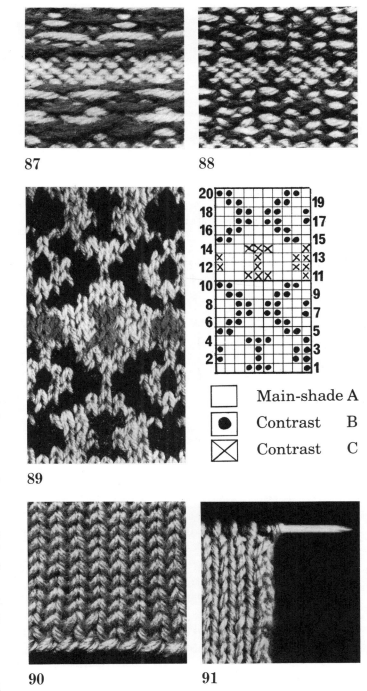

87

88

89

	Main-shade A
●	Contrast B
✕	Contrast C

90

91

WORK AND TWIST COLOURS TOGETHER TO CLOSE SIDE.

3rd row: [Wrong side] With contrast colour, B, work as 2nd row. DO NOT TURN WORK.

4th row: [Wrong side again] With main shade, A, work as 1st row. TURN WORK AND TWIST COLOURS TOGETHER TO CLOSE SIDE.

These four rows form patt.

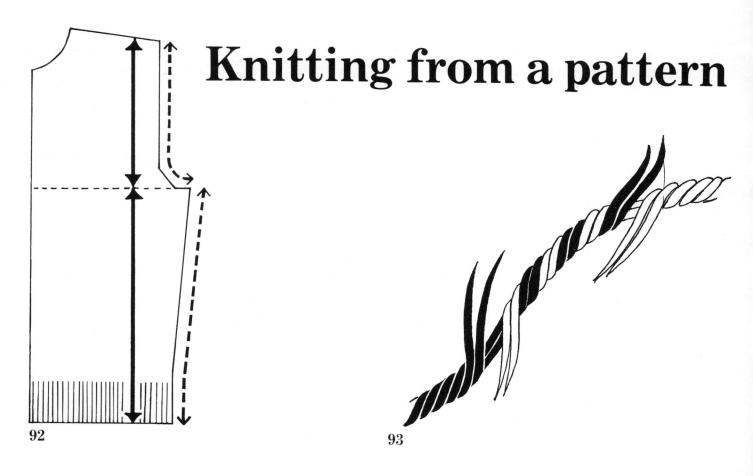

92

93

Knitting from a pattern

Materials

Once you have chosen the design you wish to make it is important to obtain the correct yarn as a garment which has been specially designed for a 4-ply wool cannot turn out correctly if you substitute a mohair or bouclé wool for example. If you cannot obtain the exact yarn you can substitute it for another yarn of the same type. For example a 4-ply wool for a 4-ply wool or a double knitting wool for a double knitting wool, as long as you make sure that the tension you obtain with the substitute is the same as that given in your pattern (see page 14). If you do not obtain the same tension try changing the needle size and if this does not work, please don't continue in the vain hope that it will be alright in the end. It won't be and you will only be disappointed with the results. You can write to the manufacturer of the particular yarn you require, asking them to give you the name of your nearest stockist.

It is also important to buy the given quantity of yarn at the same time so that you obtain the same dye lot for the whole garment, remembering that if you intend to add extra inches to the measurements you must allow for extra yarn. Keep one of the ball bands just in case you should need it, as this will ensure that you know the number of the original dye lot if you have to buy any more yarn.

Tension

Before beginning the pattern, CHECK YOUR TENSION as given on page 15.

Measurements

Nearly all patterns give instructions for more than one size, with the first set of figures referring to the smallest size and figures for larger sizes given in brackets, thus, 32″ (34″–36″–38″) bust. Based on these sizes, if you are making a garment in a 36″ bust size, the number of stitches and measurements for your size will be shown as the

34

second set of figures in brackets throughout, unless only one set of figures is given, which will apply to all sizes. Before you begin knitting you may find it easier to go through the pattern and underline all the figures given for your size. Measurements for body and sleeve lengths will be given in the pattern and if you want to add to any of these measurements, always remember to allow for extra yarn.

Knitting should be placed on a flat surface and measurements should be taken in the centre of the work and not at the edges (fig. 92). Adjustments can be made to the length of the body by adding or taking away rows before the armhole shaping is reached. Where there is side shaping on the body or sleeves, adjust the length when the shaping has been completed. Be very accurate about measuring armhole depth; never measure on the side curve and never try to alter the length here if possible (see 'Making Adjustments to Patterns', page 36), as the correct fit of the sleeves depends on the correct armhole depth. Remember to work the same number of rows on pieces which have to be joined, for example, the front and back of a garment; a row counter can be very useful here.

Joining in a new ball

Always join in a new ball of yarn at the beginning of a row, if possible. You can gauge whether you have sufficient yarn for another row by spreading out your work and checking whether the yarn will cover its width four times. Any odd lengths of yarn can be saved for sewing up. If the yarn has to be joined in the middle of the work, which is necessary when working on circular needles, the ends should be spliced. Unravel the ends of yarn of the ball being used and the new ball, cut away one or two strands from each end, overlay the two ends and twist together until they hold. The twisted ends should be of the same thickness as the original yarn. Knit very carefully with the newly twisted yarn for a few stitches, then trim away the odd ends of yarn. If you cannot join the yarn at the beginning of a row,

never knit a knot into your work but splice the ends as described (fig. 93).

Keeping work clean

A polythene bag pinned over the finished work and moved up as it grows will help to keep your knitting clean. Never stick the needles through the ball of yarn as this splits the yarn, and never leave your work in the middle of a row; you will find that this leaves a mark when you continue to knit.

Mistakes

Mistakes happen to the best knitters. If you notice a wrong stitch a row or two down, don't panic and pull the work off your needles. It may be possible to correct the mistake by dropping the stitch above it off the needle, letting it run down, then picking it up in the correct pattern with a crochet hook. Even if it is not as simple as this, careful unpicking by putting the needle into the row underneath and undoing the stitch above until you are back to the incorrect row may be better than ripping out. Always have a crochet hook on hand to pick up the dropped stitches.

Patterned stitches

The number of stitches cast on for each piece are calculated to fit the pattern exactly, so that for the first few rows you can follow the instructions without any alterations and get to know the pattern sequence. As soon as you start any shaping, however, the beginnings and ends of the pattern rows will change. With patterns made up from basic knitting and purling this is no problem, as you can see how you work each stitch from what has gone before. With more elaborate patterns you should analyse how the stitch works, then work in your extra stitches accordingly. With complicated lace stitches it may be best to work the increased stitches in stocking stitch or garter stitch until there are sufficient extra stitches to work another complete pattern. Keep a check on rows with a row counter so that you know exactly which pattern row you are working and when the next piece of shaping is due.

Making adjustments to patterns

Until you are fairly experienced in knitting it is advisable to find a pattern in the size you require. Most designs are worked out to standard dressmaking measurements, but once you have become adept at reading knitting instructions it is possible to alter them to suit your particular shape. The simplest way of making a garment one size smaller or larger is to use needles one size smaller or larger than those stated in the pattern; remember that a stitch sample must be worked before you begin, to make sure that the resulting fabric is not too tight or too loose. If this isn't successful then stitches have to be added to, or subtracted from, those given for the size nearest to your own measurements. For example if the sweater you would like to make only goes up to a 40″ chest, and you would like to make a 42″ chest size, first look at the TENSION paragraph and find out how many stitches are given to the inch. Secondly, if a patterned stitch is being used, check the number of stitches used for each pattern repeat. Using these two figures, extra stitches can be cast on for the Back and Front, or in the case of a Cardigan, halve the number of stitches cast on for the Back between the Left and Right Front. For example, if the number of stitches given for the TENSION is 7 to the inch, but the pattern is made up of 8 sts, it is much easier to add or subtract 8 sts, so that the pattern rows are worked out easily and exactly. When you have worked out the number of stitches to be cast on, work as given in the instructions, noting that any extra stitches must be included in any shaping you work, until the armholes are reached. At the armhole, decrease *half* the extra stitches equally at each side, then divide the remaining extra stitches into three, casting off one-third for each shoulder and one-third for the neck. The sleeves can be altered in the same way, decreasing half the extra stitches at each side at the beginning of the top shaping and the remainder on the final rows of the top shaping. If you use this method you will find it easier to mark all the alterations on the pattern first, so that you can work a complete section without having to calculate as you progress.

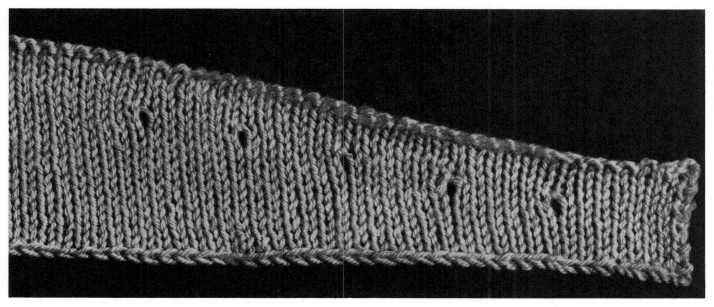

94

For a narrow-shouldered figure cast off extra stitches at the armhole and work more decreasings, but remember that there will be less stitches when you come to work the shoulder shaping.

For a full-busted figure cast on extra stitches on the front and work bust darts about $1\frac{1}{2}''$ before beginning the armhole shaping. The darts should be $1''$ from the side seams and taper to nothing about $4''$ from the edge and, once again, this is worked out from the TENSION given. For example, take a tension of 8 stitches and 10 rows to $1''$. For the *length* of the dart, take the number of stitches given to the inch and multiply by four, i.e., 32 stitches, and for the *depth* of the dart, take the number of rows to $1''$, i.e., 10 rows. Shaping should be worked on alternate rows, so on the 10 rows given the darts can be worked in five steps. On the 32 stitches given, this gives five steps of 6 stitches with two over, so the darts must be worked in four steps of 6 stitches and one of 8 stitches, thus:

1st row: Knit, or pattern, to the last 32 stitches, turn.
2nd row: Sl 1, purl or pattern to the last 32 stitches, turn.
3rd row: Sl 1, knit or pattern to the last 26 stitches, turn.
4th row: Sl 1, purl or pattern to the last 26 stitches, turn.
5th row: Sl 1, knit or pattern to the last 20 stitches, turn.
6th row: Sl 1, purl or pattern to the last 20 stitches, turn.
7th row: Sl 1, knit or pattern to the last 14 stitches, turn.
8th row: Sl 1, purl or pattern to the last 14 stitches, turn.
9th row: Sl 1, knit or pattern to the last 8 stitches, turn.
10th row: Sl 1, purl or pattern to the last 8 stitches, turn.
11th row: Sl 1, knit or pattern to the end of the row.
12th row: Sl 1, purl or pattern to the last stitch, k 1.

When the darts have been completed, work $1\frac{1}{2}''$ more, then cast off for the armholes (fig. 94). *Lengths* can be altered by adding to or taking away from the rows worked before, or after, the side shapings are worked. It is *never* advisable to alter the length after commencing the armhole shaping, as this can throw the whole design out of proportion. If, for any reason to suit your own individual measurements, the length of the armhole has to be adjusted, then remember that the sleeve top shaping must be altered accordingly.

Finishing touches

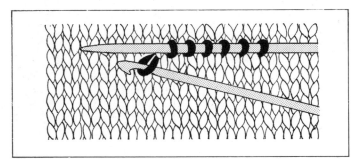

95

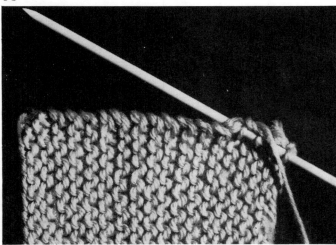

96

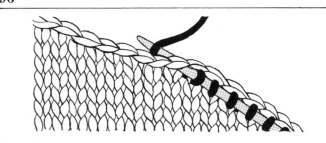

97

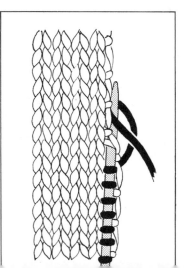

98

Edgings

Extra pieces, neckbands, pocket tops, etc., can be knitted on to the main work by picking up and knitting stitches. This gives a smooth and even line and when picked up with the right side of the fabric facing you the abbreviation is 'k up' and with the wrong side of the fabric facing you, 'p up'.

To knit up stitches across fabric have yarn on wrong side, * put a crochet hook through work from right side, pick up a loop of yarn, bring loop through to right side and slip the loop on to a knitting needle; repeat from * for the required number of stitches (fig. 95).

To knit up stitches along a straight garter stitch edge have yarn at back of work, * put knitting needle through from front to back, pick up a loop of yarn and bring loop through to right side and leave on needle; repeat from * for required number of stitches (fig. 96).

To knit up stitches round a curved edge, such as a neckline, have yarn at back of work, * put knitting needle through from front to back, pick up a loop of yarn and bring loop through to right side and leave on needle; repeat from * for required number of stitches taking care to knit up in a smooth curve (fig. 97).

To knit up stitches for front bands count the number of rows on the main fabric and check this against the number of stitches to be knitted up to make sure that you pick them up evenly. Work as given for straight garter-stitch edge (fig. 98).

Hems and Facings

These are usually worked in stocking-stitch and should always be a little narrower or finer than the main fabric, otherwise they may stretch the edge of the garment. Details of stitches and rows to be worked will be given in the instructions.

Plain hem

Beginning with a knit row, work in stocking-stitch on needles two sizes smaller than for the main fabric for the required hem length, ending with a knit row. On the next row, knit all the stitches through the back of the loop to mark the hemline. Change to required needles for the main fabric and either begin with a knit row for stocking-stitch or work the first row of the pattern for the main stitch. When work is completed turn the hem to the wrong side at the marked hemline and slip stitch to the wrong side (fig. 99) taking great care to stitch along the straight line of knitting (fig. 100).

99

100

Picot hem

This makes a pretty finish to any garment. Work required hem depth in stocking-stitch as given for plain hem, ending with a purl row. Next row: * knit 2 together, yarn forward between needles and over right-hand needle to make a stitch; repeat from * to end or, for an odd number of stitches, repeat from * to last stitch, knit 1. This makes a row of holes (fig. 101). Beginning with a purl row continue in stocking-stitch. When work is finished fold hem along centre of picot row to wrong side and slip stitch (fig. 102).

101

Knitted-up hems

This can be done for both the plain and picot hems described above and leaves virtually no mark on the right side. Cast on by the loop method given on page 8 and work the plain or picot hem as given. Work exactly the same number of rows above the hemline, ending with a purl row. If the casting on is loose enough these stitches can be picked up with a third needle pointed at both ends, taking care that you pick up the exact number of stitches, or unravel the cast on stitches and place each stitch on a third needle. Fold up the hem to the wrong side and knit together one stitch from each needle, i.e., putting the right-hand needle through the stitch on the needle nearest to you, then through the corresponding stitch on the third needle and knit both stitches together (fig. 103).

102

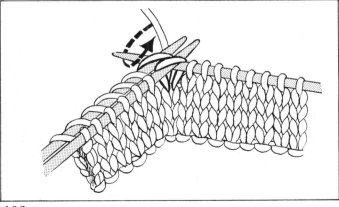

103

Finishing touches

Knitted facings

Knitted facings worked in one with main fabric, such as button and buttonhole bands. If working a buttonhole band the pattern will tell you the correct number of stitches to cast on. As an example, working from the front edge to side edge, knit 4 stitches, cast off 3 stitches, knit 4 stitches including the stitch already on right-hand needle, slip next stitch purlwise, knit 4 stitches, cast off 3 stitches, knit to end of row. On the next row purl to end including the slipped stitch, casting on two lots of 3 stitches above those cast off on the previous row (fig. 104).

Buttonholes

Your pattern will tell you how and when to work buttonholes. If you wish to change their size you can do so by adding or taking away stitches to be cast off on the armhole side of a horizontal buttonhole, or by changing the number of rows worked on a vertical buttonhole. For a very small buttonhole, make a hole in the desired position by working two stitches together then put the yarn forward and over, or round the needle to make a stitch, before working to the end of the row.

Horizontal buttonholes

Cast off the required number of stitches rather loosely. When you have cast off these stitches you will have one stitch left on the right-hand needle. Unless otherwise stated, this stitch is counted as part of the row and not part of the buttonhole, that is to say, in a row of 8 stitches with a 4 stitch buttonhole, the instructions will read: knit or pattern 2 stitches, cast off 4 stitches, knit or pattern 2 stitches, although one of the last two stitches has already been worked. In the following row, cast on the same number of stitches above those cast off in the previous row using the loop method (fig. 105).

Vertical buttonholes

The number of stitches are divided on each side of the buttonhole position, worked

104

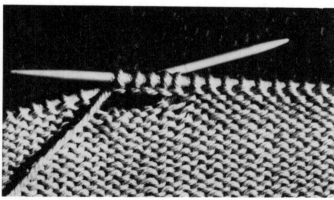

105

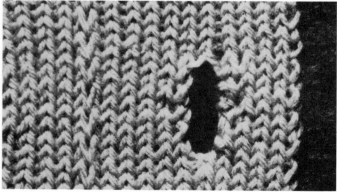

106

separately to the desired size, then rejoined. Leave the broken end of yarn for working buttonhole stitch round the buttonhole afterwards (fig. 106).

Separate front bands
When separate bands are worked for the front of a cardigan and sewn on afterwards, save time by working both bands together using separate balls of yarn. Each time you make a buttonhole, mark the other band with coloured thread; you will then know where to sew on the buttons for a perfect match.

Knitting with beads and embroidery
Your pattern will tell you the number of beads or sequins and the size required. To thread the desired number of beads on to an ounce of yarn before beginning to knit with this, fold a 10″ strand of sewing cotton in half and thread a fine needle with *both* cut ends, leaving a loop of cotton. Pass 6″ end of yarn to be used through the loop of cotton and slide beads on to the needle, down the cotton and on to the yarn. When knitting with this beaded yarn, slip bead up close to work, knit next stitch through the back of the loop in usual way pushing bead through stitch to front of work with the loop of the stitch. This allows beads to lie flat (fig. 107). The procedure is exactly the same when knitting with sequins.

Swiss darning
This is the easiest form of embroidery for use on knitted solid fabrics, such as stocking stitch. The working method is shown in figs. 108, 109 and 110, where it can be seen that the embroidery yarn merely covers a series of knitted stitches.
The same ply yarn as the knitted fabric should be used for the embroidery to ensure that the knitted stitches are completely covered.
Begin by threading a blunt needle with the embroidery yarn, and inserting the needle from the back to the front at the centre of the

107

108

109

Finishing touches

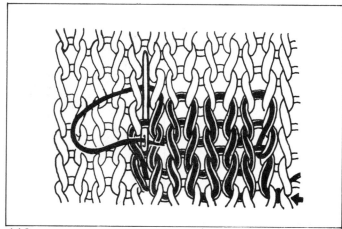

110

111

112

113

stitch (fig. 108), leaving an end on the wrong side which later can be sewn in. Now insert the needle as shown on figs. 108 and 109 through both strands of the stitch above. The arrow on fig. 109 shows the position for inserting the needle for the following stitch. Continue in this manner to cover a row of stitches.

Fig. 110 shows the embroidery carried over several rows of knitting. To continue on the row above, insert the needle under the head of the stitch, turn the work upside down and continue in the opposite direction over the following row.

It is important that the embroidery should be the same tension as the knitted fabric to prevent any distortion, and care should be taken that the knitted stitches are covered.

Lace edgings

To get the best results from these delicate edgings it is best to work them in either cotton or fine yarn with fine needles. They usually have a straight edge which is attached to the garment you are making, and are ideal finishes for articles such as fabric table cloths, table mats, pillow slips, and even sheets. The width of the edging is determined by the pattern rows but the length depends on the number of rows worked and can therefore be any length you wish. You will find that 'y fwd' is used frequently in these patterns. These are always treated as extra stitches, unless otherwise stated in the pattern, and will therefore be allowed for in the following rows; so be careful not to drop these extra stitches and do count your stitches carefully. You will find yourself in difficulties if you accidentally 'lose' these stitches.

Crystal Edging (fig. 111)
Cast on 18 sts.
Preparation row: [Wrong side] K 6, p 7, k 5.
1st row: Sl 1, k 2, y fwd, k 2 tog, k 2, k 2 tog, y fwd, k 5, y fwd, k 2 tog, [y fwd, k 1] twice.
2nd row: K 6, y fwd, k 2 tog, p 7, k 2, y fwd, k 2 tog, k 1.
3rd row: Sl 1, k 2, y fwd, k 2 tog, k 1, [k 2 tog, y fwd]

twice, k 4, y fwd, k 2 tog, [y fwd, k 1] twice, k 2.
4th row: K 8, y fwd, k 2 tog, p 7, k 2, y fwd, k 2 tog, k 1.
5th row: Sl 1, k 2, y fwd, k 2 tog, [k 2 tog, y fwd] 3 times, k 3, y fwd, k 2 tog, [y fwd, k 1] twice, k 4.
6th row: K 10, y fwd, k 2 tog, p 7, k 2, y fwd, k 2 tog, k 1.
7th row: Sl 1, k 2, y fwd, k 2 tog, k 1, [k 2 tog, y fwd] twice, k 4, y fwd, k 2 tog, [y fwd, k 1] twice, k 6.
8th row: Cast off 8, k 3, y fwd, k 2 tog, p 7, k 2, y fwd, k 2 tog, k 1. These eight rows form patt and are rep for length required.

Loop edging (fig. 112)
Cast on 11 sts.
Preparation row: K.
1st row: K 3, [y fwd, sl 1, k 1, psso, k 1] twice, [y fwd] twice, k 1, [y fwd] twice, k 1.
2nd row: [K 2, p 1] 4 times, k 3. (On this row each double y fwd is treated as 2 sts, the first being knitted, the second purled).
3rd row: K 3, y fwd, sl 1, k 1, psso, k 1, y fwd, sl 1, k 1, psso, k 7.
4th row: Cast off 4 sts, k 3, p 1, k 2, p 1, k 3.
These four rows form patt and are rep for length required.

Shark's tooth edging (fig. 113)
Cast on 8 sts.
Preparation row: K.
1st row: Sl 1, k 1, [y fwd, k 2 tog] twice, y fwd, k 2.
2nd row: K 2, y fwd, k 2, [y fwd, k 2 tog] twice, k 1.
3rd row: Sl 1, k 1, [y fwd, k 2 tog] twice, k 2, y fwd, k 2.
4th row: K 2, y fwd, k 4, [y fwd, k 2 tog] twice, k 1.
5th row: Sl 1, k 1, [y fwd, k 2 tog] twice, k 4, y fwd, k 2.
6th row: K 2, y fwd, k 6, [y fwd, k 2 tog] twice, k 1.
7th row: Sl 1, k 1, [y fwd, k 2 tog] twice, k 6, y fwd, k 2.
8th row: K 2, y fwd, k 8, [y fwd, k 2 tog] twice, k 1.
9th row: Sl 1, k 1, [y fwd, k 2 tog] twice, k 8, y fwd, k 2.
10th row: K 2, y fwd, k 10, [y fwd, k 2 tog] twice, k 1.
11th row: Sl 1, k 1, [y fwd, k 2 tog] twice, k 10, y fwd, k 2.
12th row: Cast off 11 sts, k 2, [y fwd, k 2 tog] twice, k 1.
These 12 rows form patt and are rep for length required.

Crochet in knitting
Many knitting patterns include crochet buttons and edgings in the making-up instructions. Although this book is dealing with knitting techniques we have included instructions for working some crochet to help you with your knitting patterns. For the complete

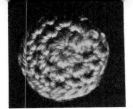

114

115

116

novice who is unable to understand the instructions given below we suggest that they seek the advice from a crochet guide or person who can crochet. The instructions below are very simple and will only take a short time to master. Abbreviations are shown on page 7.

Round buttons (fig. 114)
Work 3 chain and join into a circle with a sl st.
1st round: Work 6 dc into circle, join with a sl st into first dc.
2nd round: Work 2 dc into each dc of previous round, joining with a sl st into first dc. Rep this round until button mould is covered.
Last round: * Miss 1 dc, 1 dc into next dc; rep from * to end, joining with a sl st into first dc. Slip crochet cover over button mould and draw together under button, leaving an end of yarn for sewing on button. An additional trim may be added by working an additional row of sl st around outer edge of button after cover has been made.

Small picot edging (fig. 115)
Make a chain of multiples of 6 plus 2, turn.
1st row: 1 dc into 2nd ch from hook, * 2 ch, miss 2 ch, 1 dc into next ch; rep from * to end, 1 ch, turn.
2nd row: * 1 dc into space, 3 ch, 1 sl st into first of these 3 ch to form a picot, 1 dc into same space, 1 dc into next dc, 2 ch, miss 2 ch, 1 dc into next dc; rep from * to end.

Scallop edging (fig. 116)
Make a chain of multiples of 6, turn.
1st row: * Miss 2 ch, work 5 tr into next ch, miss 2 ch, 1 sl st into next ch; rep from * to end.

Making up knitted garments

Most reliable patterns give detailed pressing and making up instructions and it is essential to spend plenty of time on this most important part of your work; with practise you will soon produce garments with a professional finish. Remember too, that when you have finished knitting you have made your own fabric which then has to be made up like any other piece of fabric.

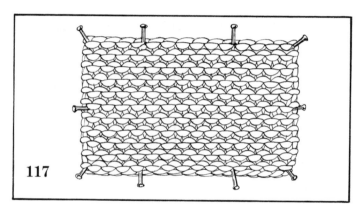

117

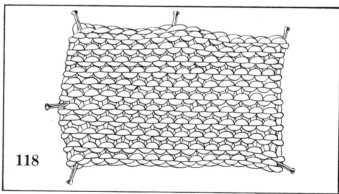

118

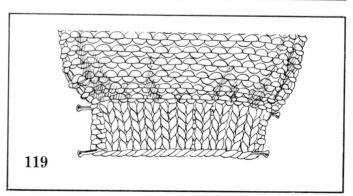

119

When pressing is directed, correctly place each *right* side down on to a well-padded surface, taking care to keep the stitches and rows running in straight lines (fig. 117). Do not stretch any part of the fabric or pin out incorrectly (fig. 118). Do not, at first, press ribbed borders but press the main part of each piece as given in the instructions. Wait until the fabric has cooled then take out the pins. If there is a ribbed border, push the ribbing together so that only the knitted stitches show and pin as illustrated, then press as given in the instructions (fig. 119). Use a blunt-ended wool needle and the original yarn for sewing together. If the yarn is not suitable for sewing, use a 3-ply yarn in the same shade. Joining seams is largely a matter of individual choice but the two methods most often used are the woven flat seam and the backstitch seam.

Woven flat seam

If you have slipped the first stitch and knitted the last stitch on every row, you will find you have a small 'pip' at the end of every two rows. With the right sides of the work facing each other, place your finger between the two pieces to be joined, insert the needle from the front through both pieces below the corresponding 'pips'; pull the yarn through and insert the needle from the back through both pieces of fabric, and pull the yarn through. The stitch should be the length of a small running stitch. Repeat this along the seam matching the 'pips' on each piece. The seam will then be drawn together and will be flat and very neat when pressed. This method is always used for baby garments, ribbing and underclothes (fig. 120).

Backstitch seam

This method is firm, yet elastic, and it keeps the garment in shape and will not break if roughly treated. Place the two pieces to be joined right sides together, join in the sewing yarn by making three small running stitches over each other, one stitch in from the edge.

Put the needle back into the beginning of the running stitch and pull the yarn through; insert the needle from the back through the fabric and beyond the first running stitch the length of another small stitch and pull the yarn through. Repeat this along the seam, keeping stitches neat and even and one stitch in from the edge of both pieces of fabric, taking care not to split the knitted stitches (fig. 121). Your pattern will tell you which seams to sew first but they are usually worked in the following order:

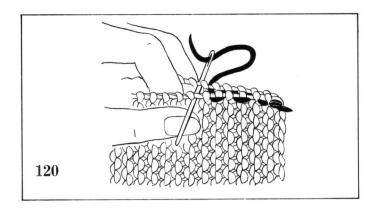

120

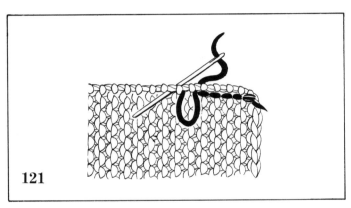

121

Shoulder seams

Backstitch firmly one stitch from the edge, taking the stitching across the steps of shaping in a straight line. Press on the wrong side. For heavy sweaters, reinforce these seams with ribbon or tape.

Set-in sleeves

Mark centre top of sleeve and pin in position to shoulder seam, then pin cast-off stitches to cast-off underarm stitches of body. Keeping the sleeve smooth on either side of the shoulder seam, work fine backstitch round the curves as near the edge as possible.

Side and sleeve seams

Join with backstitch in one complete seam as near the edge as possible.

Sewing on collars

Place right side of collar to wrong side of neck, matching centre backs and taking care not to stretch the neckline. Join with a firm backstitch as near the edge as possible.

Making up knitted garments

Helpful hints in making up
Sewn-on bands
For sewn-on bands worked separately, use a woven flat seam matching row for row.

Sewn-on pockets or any applied band or decoration
Use slip stitching, taking care to keep the line absolutely straight. A good way to ensure a straight sewing line is to thread a fine knitting needle, pointed at both ends, under every alternate stitch of the line you wish to follow and catch one stitch from the edge of the piece to be applied and one stitch from the needle alternately, using matching yarn (fig. 122).

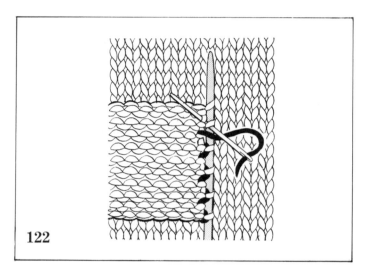

122

Sewing hems
To sew hems which have not already been knitted up (as shown on page 39) use a fine slip stitch, matching stitch for stitch (fig. 123).

Skirt waist
For a skirt waist using casing, or herringbone stitch, cut elastic to the size required and join into a circle. Mark off the waistline of the skirt and the elastic into quarters and pin the elastic into position on the wrong side, taking care to distribute the knitting evenly. Hold the knitting over the fingers of the left hand and with the elastic slightly stretched, work a herringbone stitch, catching the elastic above and below as you work (fig. 124).

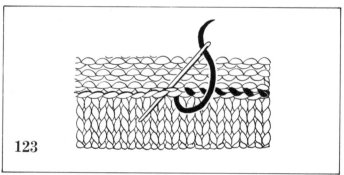

123

Ribbon facing
Lightly press the part to be faced before sewing on the ribbon, taking care not to stretch the edge. Choose a soft ribbon, available in a wide selection of colours and widths from most stores. When facing buttonhole bands, the ribbon should be wide enough to cover the strip with $\frac{1}{4}''$ to $\frac{1}{2}''$ to spare on either side and a $\frac{1}{2}''$ hem top and bottom. Take great care not to stretch the knitting when measuring the ribbon lengths, and cut the facing for buttonhole and button bands at the same time, so that they match exactly. Fold in the turnings, pin ribbon to the wrong side,

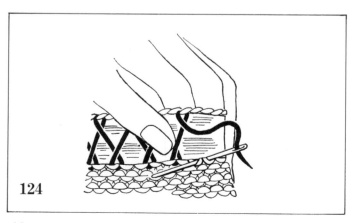

124

easing the knitting evenly; check that the buttonholes are evenly spaced. With matching silk, slip stitch with the smallest possible stitches along all edges. Cut buttonholes along the straight grain of the ribbon, remembering to make them wide enough for the buttons. Oversew the ribbon and knitting together to avoid fraying, then neaten by working button-hole stitch round the buttonhole with the original yarn (fig. 125).

Grosgrain ribbon can be shaped to fit a curved edge by pressing with a hot iron and gently stretching one edge until the desired curve is made.

When facing with ribbon on two edges at right angles, seam outside edge in place first, then fold ribbon into a mitred corner before seaming inside edge (fig. 126).

Net can be used for facings, as it is very light but has just enough body for the hem of a skirt. Cut the net three times the required depth and fold in three lengthwise. Pin to the wrong side of the part to be faced, turning up two rows of the knitting if it is in stocking-stitch, and slip stitch top and bottom.

Decorative seam

Lapped seams can be used on yokes and square-set sleeves when a firm fabric stitch has been knitted. Place the parts to be joined right sides together, with the underneath part projecting $\frac{1}{2}''$ beyond the upper part. Backstitch along edge, turn to the right side and backstitch $\frac{1}{2}''$ from the first seam through both thicknesses of fabric, taking care to keep the line of stitching straight and even.

Shrinking

Provided 100% pure wool has been used, parts of garments which have stretched can be shrunk back into place. Place the part to be shrunk face down on to a well padded surface, pat and pin into shape and size required. Cover with a really wet cloth and hold a hot iron over the cloth to make plenty of steam. Alternately steam then pat into shape, taking out the pins as soon as possible, until the required shape is achieved, then leave without handling until quite dry.

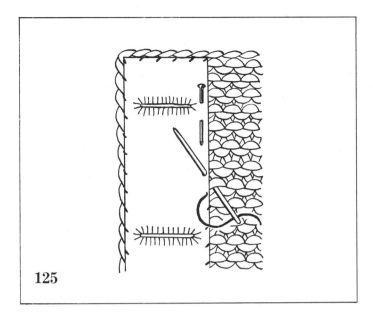

125

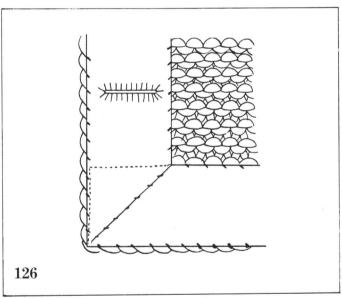

126

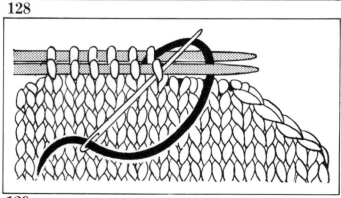

127

128

129

Making up knitted garments

Sewing in zip fasteners

Pin the zip into the opening, taking great care not to stretch the knitting. Sew in zip using backstitch, keeping the grain of the knitting straight. Except on very heavy garments, it is better to use Nylon zips as they are lighter and more flexible (fig. 127).

Skirt lining

It is generally accepted that it is better not to line a knitted skirt but to wear a waist-length petticoat. If you are unable to purchase this ready-made, buy lining material the exact shade of your skirt, press the knitted pieces and cut lining pieces to match the skirt, allowing extra width for waist seams and hems. Pin waist darts in lining to fit knitting, stitch darts, sew seams and hem; turn in the seam allowance at the top and oversew to the skirt waist. Finish with a petersham waistband, hooks and eyes and sew in a zip fastener. Do not sew the lining to seams or hem of the knitted skirt.

Elasticated knitting

Better-fitting welts and sock tops can be made by weaving shirring elastic into the knitted fabric on the wrong side of the work. This method can be used for any stitch but it works particularly well in k 1, p 1 rib. If matching elastic is used it is practically invisible.

Elasticated k 1, p 1 rib

Cast on an even number of stitches. Join elastic at end of row and hold slightly stretched over index finger of left hand.

1st row: [Right side] Hold elastic at back of work, * put point of right-hand needle through front of next stitch under elastic and k 1, yarn forward, p 1 in normal way, yarn back; repeat from * to end of row.
2nd row: Hold elastic to front of work, * put point of

right-hand needle over elastic and into front of next stitch and k 1, yarn forward, put point of right-hand needle purlwise through next stitch and under elastic and p 1, yarn back; repeat from * to end. Adjust tension, twist elastic and yarn, turn. Repeat these two rows (fig. 128).

Elastic can also be added by darning in on the wrong side of the work when garment is finished.

Grafting stitches

This means the joining of two sets of stitches, horizontally and invisibly. Here we give you the method of joining two pieces of fabric worked in stocking-stitch. The pieces should each contain the same number of stitches and should be arranged on needles of the size used for the knitting of the fabric. Break off the yarn from the last piece worked leaving an end approximately one-and-a-half times the length of the row to be worked. Place *wrong* sides together with the needle points facing to the right. Using a blunt-ended wool needle threaded with the end of yarn, work as follows. * Insert sewing needle *knitwise* through the first stitch on the front needle, draw yarn through and slip stitch off knitting needle; insert sewing needle *purlwise* through next stitch on front needle, draw yarn through and leave stitch on knitting needle; insert sewing needle *purlwise* through first stitch on back needle, draw yarn through and slip stitch off knitting needle; insert sewing needle *knitwise* through next stitch on back needle, draw yarn through and leave on knitting needle; repeat from * until all stitches are worked off both needles. Before sewing in end of yarn, it may be necessary to pull the stitches with the sewing needle until they are all of an even depth and the join looks invisible. This method of joining is usually used for the toes of socks (fig. 129).

Pure wool

Although many hand-knitting wools are now given shrink-resist finishes, the structure of hand-knitted fabrics makes elementary care in washing essential if the best results are to be obtained. If hand-knitted garments are never allowed to become badly soiled they will be easily washable, and it is important to remember that pure wool stays clean longest.

Washing should be done in warm, *not* hot, water. Detergents and soap powders should always be dissolved completely and never brought into direct contact with the garments. Rubbing should be avoided and the lather gently squeezed through the fibres. All traces of soap or detergent should be rinsed out in tepid water. A loose wringer or a spin dryer may be used to remove surplus water. Wringing by hand should be avoided. The garment should then be arranged on a clean smooth surface and gently eased into its original shape. If it is finally dried on a clothes horse the sleeves should not be allowed to hang down. When dry, the garment should be lightly pressed on the wrong side with a warm iron over a damp cloth.

Nylon

Wash often—wash soon. Nylon garments can be washed by hand or by machine. Use hot water (60°C, 140°F) for 'whites', and hand-hot (48°C, 118°F) for 'coloureds'. Use a synthetic detergent in hard water districts and dissolve thoroughly. Rinse until the water is clear. Do not wring knitwear but squeeze and dry flat. If spin drying is required, stop after the first rush of water from the outlet ceases.

Other man-made fibres

Warm wash (40°C) as soon as the garment gets soiled. Use a soapless detergent or, if your water is soft, soap flakes or powder dissolved in water pleasantly hot to the hand. Rinse thoroughly. Remove excess moisture by squeezing lightly, or rolling in a towel, or giving it a short spin dry. Finally, smooth garment and dry flat away from direct heat. Courtelle garments can be machine-washed, following instructions for delicate fabrics. When the garment is completely dry, fold neatly and store in a drawer, not on a hanger.

If absolutely necessary, synthetics may be pressed with a cool iron and a dry cloth.

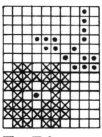

⊠ B ⊡ C

Embroidered jacket

Shown on front cover

Instructions are for a 32″ bust. Changes for 34″ and 36″ sizes are given in brackets.

MATERIALS: 5(5–6) ozs of Jaeger Celtic Spun in main shade, A; 2(2–2) ozs each in contrasting colours B and C. One pair each Nos 9 and 11 needles. Four press studs.

MEASUREMENTS: To fit a 32″(34″–36″) bust. Length at centre back: 19″(19½–20″).

TENSION: 6 sts and 8 rows to 1″ over st-st on No 9 needles.

LEFT FRONT: With No 11 needles and B cast on 95(101–107) sts. **1st row:** With B, k 2, * p 1, k 1; rep from * to last st, k 1. **2nd row:** With B, * k 1, p 1; rep from * to last st, k 1. **3rd row:** With C, as 1st row. **4th row:** With C, as 2nd row. Rep these four rows 4 times more. [Do not break wool when changing colour but carry it up the side of the work when not in use.] Change to No 9 needles and cont with A. **Next row:** K to last 18 sts, turn leaving these 18 sts on a holder. **Next row:** P. Cont on rem 77(83–89) sts. **1st row:** K to last 2 sts, k 2 tog. **2nd row:** P. Rep these 2 rows 26(28–30) times more. 50(54–58) sts. **Commence sleeve. Next row:** Cast on 6 sts, k to last 2 sts, k 2 tog. Keeping sleeve edge straight cont to dec at centre front edge on every alt row until 33(36–39) sts rem, then on every foll 4th row until 27(30–33) sts rem. Work 5(3–1) rows without shaping, ending at sleeve edge. **Shape shoulder.** Keeping neck edge straight, cast off 6(6–6) sts at beg of next row, and 5(6–7) sts at beg of foll 3 alt rows. Work 1 row. Cast off 6(6–6) rem sts.

RIGHT FRONT: With No 11 needles and B cast on 95(101–107) sts. Work 20 rows in ribbing as given for Left Front. **Next row:** Rib 18 sts and sl on to a holder. Change to No 9 needles, and with A, k to end. **Next row:** P. Cont as folls: **1st row:** K 2 tog, k to end. **2nd row:** P. Rep 1st and 2nd rows 26(28–30) times more, then 1st row once. **Commence sleeve. Next row:** Cast on 6 sts, p to end. Complete to match Left Front, working one more row before commencing shoulder shaping.

BACK: With No 11 needles and B, cast on 89(95–101) sts. Work 20 rows in ribbing as for Left Front. Change to No 9 needles and cont with A in st-st. Work until back measures same as fronts to beg of sleeves, ending with a p row. **Commence sleeves.** Cast on 6 sts at beg of next 2 rows. Work until sleeve edge measures same as fronts, ending with a p row. **Shape shoulders and back of neck. Next row:** Cast off 6(6–6) sts, k 28(31–34) sts including st on needle, cast off 33(33–33) sts, k to end. Cont on last set of sts as folls: **1st row:** Cast off 6(6–6) sts, p to last 2 sts, p 2 tog. **2nd row:** K 2 tog, k to end. **3rd row:** Cast off 5(6–7) sts, p to last 2 sts, p 2 tog. Rep 2nd and 3rd rows twice more. Work 1 row. Cast off 6(6–6) rem sts. Rejoin wool to rem sts at neck edge. **1st row:** P 2 tog, p to end. **2nd row:** Cast off 5(6–7) sts, k to last 2 sts, k 2 tog. Rep 1st and 2nd rows twice more and then 1st row once. Cast off rem 6(6–6) sts.

LEFT FRONT BORDER: Sl sts from holder on to a No 11 needle and rejoin B. **1st row:** [Right side] Cast on one st, rib to end. Cont in rib and stripes on these 19 sts until border is long enough to fit along centre-front edge, and along back edge to centre of neck. Cast off firmly in rib.

RIGHT FRONT BORDER: Work as for Left Front Border, noting that first row is wrong side.

SLEEVE BORDERS: With No 11 needles and B, cast on 19 sts. Work in striped ribbing as for Left Front. Work until border is long enough to fit along sleeve edge, ending with a stripe in C. Cast off in rib.

TO MAKE UP: Press each piece lightly with warm iron and damp cloth. Sew shoulder seams. Join cast off edges of front borders neatly. Place seam at centre back of neck and sew borders to front and neck edges. Sew borders to sleeve edge. Sew side and undersleeve seams. Press seams. Sew two press studs to Left side seam on the outside at top and bottom of welt, and two press studs to right side seam on the inside in same way. Sew other halves of press studs to edges of front welts to match. Embroider motifs from chart as required *(see Swiss darning on page 41, which will show you how to embroider on knitted fabric).*

Butterfly vest

Instructions are for a 34″ bust. Changes for 36″ and 38″ sizes are given in brackets.

MATERIALS: 8(8–9) ozs of Lee Target Motoravia 4-ply in Main shade, A. 2 ozs of same in contrast, B; 1 oz each of same in contrasts C and D. One pair each Nos 10 and 11 needles. A No 11 (International size 3·00) crochet hook.

MEASUREMENTS: To fit a 34″(36″–38″) bust. Length from shoulder: 26″(26″–26¼″).

TENSION: 7 sts and 8½ rows to 1″ over st-st on No 10 needles.

NOTE: Use a separate ball of wool for each part of the patt and ensure that wools are twisted tog when changing colour to avoid holes. If preferred the wings can be knitted completely in the first contrasting colour and the 2nd and 3rd colours embroidered afterwards.

FRONT: With No 11 needles and A, cast on 128(134–140) sts. Beg with a k row, work 11 rows st-st. K next row to form hemline. Change to No 10 needles. Beg with a k row cont in st-st. Work 2 rows. ** **Next row:** K 9(12–15) A, * 3B, 26A, 3B, 7A; rep from * ending last rep k 9(12–15) A instead of 7A. [This is first row of chart] Cont working 3 butterflies from chart with the main part of work in A. Work 2 rows in A. ** Rep from ** to ** 4 times more. [5 rows of butterflies in all]. **Work yoke.** Cont in A only. **Next row:** K 3(6–3) sts, * p 2, k 2; rep from * to last 5(8–5) sts, p 2, k 3(6–3). **Next row:** P 3(6–3) sts, * k 2, p 2; rep from * to last 5(8–5) sts, k 2, p 3(6–3). These 2 rows form yoke patt. Work 4 more rows. **Shape armholes.** Cast off 8(10–10) sts at beg of next 2 rows. Dec 1 st at each end of every foll row until 102(104–110) sts rem, then one st at each end of every alt row until 94(94–98) sts rem. Cont without shaping until armhole measures 3¼″(3¼″–3½″) from beg, measured on straight, ending with a right side row. **Shape neck. Next row:** Patt 33(33–33) sts, cast off 28(28–32) sts, patt to end. Complete each side separately. Keeping armhole edge straight, dec 1 st at neck edge on every row 6 times, then 1 st on every alt row 5 times. Cont without shaping until armhole measures 6¾″(6¾″–7″) from beg, measured on straight, ending at armhole edge. **Shape shoulder.** Keeping neck edge straight, cast off at beg of next and alt rows at shoulder edge, 8(8–8) sts once and 7(7–7) sts twice. Rejoin wool to rem sts at neck edge and complete to match first side working 1 more row before commencing shoulder shaping.

BACK: Work as for Front until armhole shaping is complete. Work until armholes measure 6¼″(6¼″–6½″) from beg, ending with a right side row. **Shape neck. Next row:** Patt 24(24–24) sts, cast off 46(46–50) sts, patt to end. Complete each side separately. **1st row:** Patt to last 2 sts, dec 1 st. **2nd row:** Dec 1 st, patt to end. **Shape shoulder.** Keeping neck edge straight, cast off at beg of next and foll alt rows at shoulder edge, 8(8–8) sts once and 7(7–7) sts twice. Rejoin wool to rem sts at neck edge. **1st row:** Dec 1 st, patt to end. **2nd row:** Patt to last 2 sts, dec 1 st. **3rd row:** Work in patt. Shape shoulder to match first side.

TO MAKE UP: Sew in all loose ends. Press each piece lightly with a warm iron and damp cloth. Join shoulder and side seams using back st. Turn up hem and slip st. **Neck border.** Join in A to back neck edge at right shoulder. With No 11 crochet hook, work a row of dc right round neck edge, working 1 dc for each 2 rows or 3 dc for each 4 sts. Turn with 1 ch and work another row right round. Break wool and fasten off. Join edges neatly. **Armhole borders.** Join wool to underarm at side seams and work 2 rows dc round armhole edges as for neck border. Press seams and borders lightly.

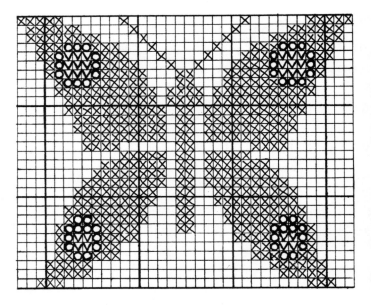

☒   B   First contrasting colour
◘   C   Second contrasting colour
☑   D   Third contrasting colour

Sequin jacket

Instructions are for a 32″ bust. Changes for 34″, 36″, 38″ and 40″ bust are given in brackets.

MATERIALS: 5(5-6-6-7) ozs of Sirdar Fontein 4-ply Crepe in main shade, A (Aubretia); 4(4-5-5-6) ozs of same in contrast, B (Silver); contrast, C (Emerald); contrast, D (Royal); 4(4-5-5-6) strings of 8 mm sequins of each colour. 1 pair each Nos 11 and 12 needles.

MEASUREMENTS: To fit a 32″(34″-36″-38″-40″) bust. Length at centre back: 23¾″(24″-24½″-24¾″-25″). Sleeve seam: 18½″.

TENSION: 8 sts and 10 rows to 1″ over sequin patt on No 11 needles.

NOTE: Thread approx 1 string of sequins on each ounce of wool. Sequins from Ells & Farrier, 5 Princes Street, London W.1.

BACK: With No 11 needles and A, cast on 127(135-143-151-159) sts. **1st row:** * K 3, push sequin close to next st, k 1 tbl, bringing sequin through to front with st as it is knitted — called S1 tbl; rep from * to last 3 sts, k 3. **2nd and every alt row:** P. **3rd row:** * K 1, S1 tbl, k 2; rep from * to last 3 sts, k 1, S1 tbl, k 1. **4th row:** P. These four rows form patt and are rep throughout working in stripes as folls: 20 rows A, 20 rows B, 20 rows C and 20 rows D. When 3rd stripe is completed (C) inc at each end of first row of every stripe until there are 137(145-153-161-169) sts. Cont without shaping until work measures 16¾″, ending with a p row. **Shape armholes.** Cast off 6(7-8-9-10) sts at beg of next 2 rows. Dec 1 st at each end of next 6 rows, then at each end of next and every foll alt row until 101 (105-109-113-117) sts rem. Cont without shaping until armholes measure 6¾″(7″-7¼″-7½″-7¾″), ending with a p row. **Shape shoulders.** Cast off at beg of next and every row 6 sts 8 times and 6(7-8-9-10) sts twice. Cast off rem 41(43-45-47-49) sts.

LEFT FRONT: With No 11 needles and A, cast on 59 (63-67-71-75) sts. Work in patt as given for Back until 3rd(C) stripe has been completed. Inc 1 st at beg of next and every foll first row of each stripe until there are 64(68-72-76-80) sts. Cont without shaping until work measures same as back to underarm, ending with a p row. **Shape armholes.** Cast off 6(7-8-9-10) sts at beg of next row. Work 1 row. Dec 1 st at armhole edge on next 6 rows, then on next and every foll alt row until 46(48-50-52-54) sts rem. Cont without shaping until armhole measures 4¾″(5″-5¼″-5½″-5¾″) ending at front edge. **Shape neck.** Cast off at beg of next and every alt row 4(5-6-6-6) sts once, 4(4-4-5-6) sts once, 3 sts twice and 2 sts once. Cont without shaping until work measures same as Back to shoulder, ending at armhole edge. **Shape shoulder.** Cast off at beg of next and alt rows 6 sts 4 times and 6(7-8-9-10) sts once.

RIGHT FRONT: Work as for Left Front reversing shaping.

SLEEVES: With No 11 needles and D cast on 63 (63-67-67-71) sts and work 1¼″ in sequin patt, inc 1 st at each end of 5th and every foll 8th row until there are 101(105-109-113-117) sts at same time cont in sequin patt stripes [of 20 rows each beg with A], then cont straight until work measures 18½″, ending on same patt row as back and sides. **Shape top.** Cast off 6(7-8-9-10) sts at beg of next 2 rows. Dec 1 st at each end of next 6 rows, then at each end of next and every foll alt row until 51 sts rem. Cast off 3 sts at beg of next 6 rows. Cast off rem sts.

TO MAKE UP: Join shoulder, side and sleeve seams using Back st. Set in sleeves. **Bands.** With No 12 needles and A, cast on 6 sts and work 2 rows in k 1, p 1 rib. Change to B and work 2 rows, then 2 rows C and 2 rows D [8 row patt]. Rep these eight rows, making bands long enough to fit round bottom, cuffs and neck and front edges, always beg and ending with A. Cast off each time in A. Pin bands in place and sew in given order, laying band under sequin knitting and working a flat seam. Very lightly press *bands* only.

Lace cardigan and skirt

Instructions are for a 34″ bust, 36″ hips. Changes for 36″ bust, 38″ hips are given in brackets.

MATERIALS: Cardigan. 17(18) ozs Jaeger Summerspun. **Skirt.** 17(18) ozs of same. One pair each Nos 11 and 13 needles. Five buttons for cardigan. Waist length of 1″ wide elastic for each skirt.

MEASUREMENTS: Cardigan. To fit a 34″(36″) bust. Length from shoulder: 29″(29¼″). Sleeve seam: 16½″ (16½″). **Skirt.** Length: 40″(40″).

TENSION: 6 sts and 8½ rows to 1″ on No 11 needles.

CARDIGAN

BACK: With No 11 needles cast on 125(133) sts. Beg with a k row, work 13 rows st-st. K next row on wrong side to mark hemline. **Next row:** K. **Next row:** P. Cont in patt. **1st row:** [Both sizes] K 1, * y fwd, sl 1, k 2 tog, psso, y fwd, k 1; rep from * to end. **2nd and every alt row:** P. **3rd row:** [Smaller size only] K 1, * y fwd, sl 1, k 2 tog, psso, y fwd, k 5; rep from * to last 4 sts, y fwd, sl 1, k 2 tog, psso, y fwd, k 1. **3rd row:** [Larger size only] K 5, * y fwd, sl 1, k 2 tog, psso, y fwd, k 5; rep from * to end. **5th row:** As 3rd row. **7th row:** [Smaller size only] K 1, * k 3, y fwd, sl 1, k 1, psso, k 1, k 2 tog, y fwd; rep from * to last 4 sts, k 4. **7th row:** [Larger size only] K 3, k 2 tog, y fwd, * k 3, y fwd, sl 1, k 1, psso, k 1, k 2 tog, y fwd; rep from * to last 8 sts, k 3, y fwd, sl 1, k 1, psso, k 3. **8th row:** P. These eight rows form patt. Work 8 more rows. Keeping patt correct, dec 1 st at each end of next row, then every foll 16th row until 109(117) sts rem. Cont until back measures 22″(22″) from hemline, ending with a p row. **Shape armholes.** Cast off at beg of next and foll rows 6(6) sts twice and 2(2) sts twice. Dec 1 st at beg of every row until 85(93) sts rem. Cont until armholes measure 6¾″(7″) measured straight, ending with a p row. **Shape shoulders.** Cast off at beg of next and foll rows 6(7) sts 6 times and 7(7) sts twice. Cast off rem 35(37) sts for back of neck.

LEFT FRONT: Pocket lining. With No 2 needles cast on 29 sts. Work 36 rows in st-st ending with a p row. Cont as folls: **1st row:** K 1, * y fwd, sl 1, k 2 tog, psso, y fwd, k 1; rep from * to end. **2nd row:** P. **3rd row:** K 5, [y fwd, sl 1, k 2 tog, psso, y fwd, k 5] 3 times. Break yarn and leave sts on holder. With No 11 needles cast on 61(65) sts. Beg with a k row work 13 rows st-st. K next row on wrong side to form hemline. **Next row:** K. **Next row:** P. Cont in patt. **1st row:** [Both sizes] K 1, * y fwd, sl 1, k 2 tog, psso, y fwd, k 1; rep from * to end. **2nd and every alt row:** P. **3rd row:** [Smaller size only] K 1, [y fwd, sl 1, k 2 tog, psso, y fwd, k 5] 3 times, y fwd, sl 1, k 2 tog, psso, y fwd, k 13, [y fwd, sl 1, k 2 tog, psso, y fwd, k 5] twice, y fwd, sl 1, k 2 tog, psso, y fwd, k 1. **3rd row:** [Larger size only] K 5, [y fwd, sl 1, k 2 tog, psso, y fwd, k 5] 3 times, y fwd, sl 1, k 2 tog, psso, y fwd, k 13, [y fwd, sl 1, k 2 tog, psso, y fwd, k 5] twice, y fwd, sl 1, k 2 tog, psso, y fwd, k 1. **5th row:** As 3rd. **7th row:** [Smaller size only] K 1, [k 3, y fwd, sl 1, k 1, psso, k 1, k 2 tog, y fwd] 3 times, k 3, y fwd, sl 1, k 1, psso, k 9, k 2 tog, y fwd, [k 3, y fwd, sl 1, k 1, psso, k 1, k 2 tog, y fwd] twice, k 4. **7th row:** [Larger size only] K 3, k 2 tog, y fwd, [k 3, y fwd, sl 1, k 1, psso, k 1, k 2 tog, y fwd] 3 times, k 3, y fwd, sl 1, k 1, psso, k 9, k 2 tog, y fwd, [k 3, y fwd, sl 1, k 1, psso, k 1, k 2 tog, y fwd] twice, k 4. **9th row:** [Smaller size only] K 1, [y fwd, sl 1, k 2 tog, psso, y fwd, k 1] 7 times, y fwd, sl 1, k 1, psso, k 7, k 2 tog, y fwd, k 1, [y fwd, sl 1, k 2 tog, psso, y fwd, k 1] 5 times. **9th row:** [Larger size only] K 1, [y fwd, sl 1, k 2 tog, psso, y fwd, k 1] 8 times, y fwd, sl 1, k 1, psso, k 7, k 2 tog, y fwd, k 1, [y fwd, sl 1, k 2 tog, psso, y fwd, k 1] 5 times. **11th row:** [Smaller size only] K 1, [y fwd, sl 1, k 2 tog, psso, y fwd, k 5] 3 times, y fwd, sl 1, k 2 tog, psso, y fwd, k 2, y fwd, sl 1, k 1, psso, k 5, k 2 tog, y fwd, k 2, [y fwd, sl 1, k 2 tog, psso, y fwd, k 5] twice, y fwd, sl 1, k 2 tog, psso, y fwd, k 1. **11th row:** [Larger size only] K 5, [y fwd, sl 1, k 2 tog, psso, y fwd, k 5] 3 times, y fwd, sl 1, k 2 tog, psso, y fwd, k 2, y fwd, sl 1, k 1, psso, k 5, k 2 tog, y fwd, k 2, [y fwd, sl 1, k 2 tog, psso, y fwd, k 5] twice y fwd, sl 1, k 2 tog, psso, y fwd, k 1. **13th row:** [Smaller size only] K 1, [y fwd, sl 1, k 2 tog, psso, y fwd, k 5] 3 times, y fwd, sl 1, k 2 tog, psso, y fwd, k 3, y fwd, sl 1, k 1, psso, k 3, k 2 tog, y fwd, k 3, [y fwd, sl 1, k 2 tog, psso, y fwd, k 5] twice, y fwd, sl 1, k 2 tog, psso, y fwd, k 1. **13th row:** [Larger size only] K 5, [y fwd, sl 1, k 2 tog, psso, y fwd, k 5) 3 times, y fwd, sl 1, k 2 tog, psso, y fwd, k 3, y fwd, sl 1, k 1, psso, k 3, k 2 tog, y fwd, k 3, [y fwd, sl 1, k 2 tog, psso, y fwd, k 5] twice, y fwd, sl 1, k 2 tog, psso, y fwd, k 1. **15th row:** [Smaller size only] K 1, [k 3, y fwd, sl 1, k 1, psso, k 1, k 2 tog, y fwd] 3 times, k 3, y fwd, sl 1, k 1, psso, k 2, y fwd, sl 1, k 1, psso, k 1, k 2 tog, y fwd, k 2, k 2 tog, y fwd, [k 3, y fwd,

Lace cardigan and skirt

sl 1, k 1, psso, k 1, k 2 tog, y fwd] twice, k 4. **15th row:** [Larger size only] K 3, k 2 tog, y fwd, [k 3, y fwd, sl 1, k 1, psso, k 1, k 2 tog, y fwd] 3 times, k 3, y fwd, sl 1, k 1, psso, k 2, y fwd, sl 1, k 1, psso, k 1, k 2 tog, y fwd, k 2, k 2 tog, y fwd, [k 3, y fwd, sl 1, k 1, psso, k 1, k 2 tog, y fwd] twice, k 4. **16th row:** P. These 16 rows form patt. Dec 1 st at beg of next row, then on foll two 16th rows. [58(62) sts] Work 1 row. **Work pocket. Next row:** Patt 17(21) sts, cast off 29 sts firmly k-wise, patt to end. **Next row:** Patt to end, working pocket lining sts in place of those cast off. Patt 12 rows. Dec 1 st at beg of next row, then every foll 16th row until 53(57) sts rem. Work until front measures 22″(22″) from hemline, ending at side edge. **Shape armhole and front. 1st row:** Cast off 6(6) sts, patt to last 2 sts, dec 1 st. **2nd row:** Work in patt. **3rd row:** Cast off 2(2) sts, patt to end. **4th row:** Work in patt. **5th row:** Dec 1 st, patt to last 2 sts, dec 1 st. **6th row:** Work in patt. **7th row:** Dec 1 st, patt to end. **8th row:** Work in patt. Rep 5th to 8th rows inclusive once more. Keeping armhole edge straight cont to dec for front on next row, then on every foll 4th row until 25(28) sts rem. Work 1 row, ending at armhole edge. **Shape shoulder.** Keeping neck edge straight, cast off at beg of next and alt rows at shoulder edge, 6(7) sts 3 times. Work 1 row. Cast off rem 7(7) sts.

RIGHT FRONT: Work pocket lining as for Left Front. With No 11 needles cast on 61(65) sts. Work hem as given for Left Front. Cont in patt. **1st row:** [Both sizes] K 1, * y fwd, sl 1, k 2 tog, psso, y fwd, k 1; rep from * to end. **2nd and every alt row:** P. **3rd row:** [Smaller size only] K 1, [y fwd, sl 1, k 2 tog, psso, y fwd, k 5] twice, y fwd, sl 1, k 2 tog, psso, y fwd, k 13, [y fwd, sl 1, k 2 tog, psso, y fwd, k 5] 3 times, y fwd, sl 1, k 2 tog, psso, y fwd, k 1. **3rd row:** [Larger size only] K 1, [y fwd, sl 1, k 2 tog, psso, y fwd, k 5] twice, y fwd, sl 1, k 2 tog, psso, y fwd, k 13, [y fwd, sl 1, k 2 tog, psso, y fwd, k 5] 4 times. This sets patt. Work 13 more rows. Dec 1 st at end of next row, then on 2 foll 16th rows. Work 1 row. **Work pocket. Next row:** Patt 12 sts, cast off 29 sts firmly k-wise, patt to end. **Next row:** Patt to end, working pocket lining sts in place of those cast off. Complete to match Left Front reversing shaping.

SLEEVES: With No 11 needles cast on 53(53) sts. Beg with a k row work 13 rows st-st. K next row to form hemline. **Next row:** K. **Next row:** P. Cont in patt. **1st row:** K 1, * y fwd, sl 1, k 2 tog, psso, y fwd, k 1; rep from * to end. **2nd and every alt row:** P. **3rd row:** K 1, [y fwd, sl 1, k 2 tog, psso, y fwd, k 5] twice, y fwd, sl 1, k 2 tog, psso, y fwd, k 13, [y fwd, sl 1, k 2 tog, psso, y fwd, k 5] twice, y fwd, sl 1, k 2 tog, psso, y fwd, k 1. This sets patt. Work 13 more rows. Inc 1 st at each end

of next and every foll 8th row until there are 69(69) sts. **Smaller size only.** Inc 1 st at each end of every 12th row, and for **larger size only** cont to inc 1 st at each end of every foll 8th row until there are 77(81) sts. Cont without shaping until sleeve measures 16½″(16½″) from hemline, ending with a p row. **Shape top.** Cast off at beg of next and foll rows, 6(6) sts twice and 2(2) sts twice. Dec 1 st at beg of every row until 33 sts rem. Cast off 2 sts at beg of next 6 rows. Cast off rem 21 sts.

BORDER: With No 13 needles cast on 25 sts. **1st row:** K 12, sl 1 p-wise with yarn at back of st, to mark folding line, k 12. **2nd row:** P. Rep 1st and 2nd rows eight times more. **Next row:** K 4, cast off 4, k 4 including st already on needle, sl 1 p-wise, k 4, cast off 4, k to end. **Next row:** P to end, casting on 4 sts over those cast off on previous row. Cont until border is long enough to fit along centre front and neck edges, making four more sets of buttonholes at 2½″ intervals. Cast off.

TO MAKE UP: Pin each piece out to size and shape and press with hot iron and damp cloth. Join shoulder seams. Set in sleeves. Join side and sleeve seams using back st. Turn up hems to wrong side and sl-st. Sew neatly round pocket linings. Sew border to front and neck edges. Fold on to wrong side and sl-st. Buttonhole st round buttonholes. Press seams. Sew on buttons to correspond with buttonholes.

SKIRT

FRONT: With No 11 needles cast on 157(165) sts. Work hem as given for Cardigan Back. Cont in patt. **1st row:** K 1, * y fwd, sl 1, k 2 tog, psso, y fwd, k 1; rep from * to end. **2nd and every alt row:** P. **3rd row:** K 1, * y fwd, sl 1, k 2 tog, psso, y fwd, k 5; rep from * to last 4 sts, y fwd, sl 1, k 2 tog, psso, y fwd, k 1. **5th row:** As 3rd. **7th row:** K 1, * k 3, y fwd, sl 1, k 1, psso, k 1, k 2 tog, y fwd; rep from * to last 4 sts, k 4. **8th row:** P. These eight rows form patt. Work 24 more rows. Keeping patt correct, dec 1 st at each end of next and every foll 12th row until 117(125) sts rem. Cont without shaping until front measures 32″(32″) from hemline, ending with a p row. Dec 1 st at each end of next and every foll 8th row until 107(115) sts rem, then 1 st at each end of every foll 4th row until 95(103) sts rem. Cont without shaping until front measures 40″ (40″) from hemline, ending with a p row. Cast off.

BACK: Work as for Front.

TO MAKE UP: Pin each piece out to size and shape. Press with hot iron and damp cloth. Join side seams using back st. Turn hem to wrong side and sl st. Press seams. Join narrow edges of elastic to form a ring, then sew one edge of elastic to waist edge of skirt. Work over the elastic in casing-st to hold it in position.

Classic cable cardigan

Instructions are for a 32″/34″ bust. Changes for 34″/36″, 36″/38″ and 38″/40″ sizes are given in brackets.

MATERIALS: 14(14–15–16) ozs of Jaeger Celtic Spun. One pair each Nos 7 and 10 needles. Six buttons.

MEASUREMENTS: To fit a 32″/34″(34″/36″–36″/38″–38″/40″) bust. Length at centre back: 28½″(28½″–28¾″–28¾″). Sleeve seam: 18″(18½″–18½″–18½″).

TENSION: 7 sts and 7½ rows to 1″ on No 7 needles.

LEFT FRONT: With No 10 needles cast on 70(74–78–82) sts. **1st row:** * P 1, k 1; rep from * to last 2 sts, p 2. **2nd row:** K 2, * p 1, k 1; rep from * to end. Rep 1st and 2nd rows once more, then 1st row once. **Next row:** K 2, * p 5, k 2 tog, k 1; rep from * to last 4(8–4–8) sts, p 4(8–4–8). [62(66–69–73) sts] Change to No 7 needles and patt. **1st row:** K 4(8–4–8) sts, p 2, * sl 1 p-wise with wool at back of st, k 4, p 2; rep from * to end. **2nd row:** K 2, * p 4, sl 1 p-wise with wool at front of st, k 2; rep from * to last 4(8–4–8) sts, p 4(8–4–8). **3rd row:** K 4(8–4–8), p 2, * drop sl st to front of work, k 2, pick up dropped st and k it, k 2, p 2; rep from * to end. **4th row:** K 2, * p 5, k 2; rep from * to last 4(8–4–8) sts, p 4(8–4–8). **5th row:** K 4(8–4–8) sts, p 2, * k 4, sl 1 p-wise with wool at back of st, p 2; rep from * to end. **6th row:** K 2, * sl 1 p-wise with wool at front of st, p 4, k 2; rep from * to last 4(8–4–8) sts, p 4(8–4–8). **7th row:** K 4(8–4–8) sts, p 2, * k 2, sl 2 p-wise with wool at back of sts, drop sl st to front of work, sl same 2 sts back to left-hand needle, pick up dropped st and k it, k 2, p 2; rep from * to end. **8th row:** As 4th. These eight rows form patt. Cont until front measures 19½″ from beg, ending with a wrong side row. **Shape front. 1st row:** Work to last 2 sts, dec 1 st. **2nd and 3rd rows:** Patt. **4th row:** Dec 1 st, patt to end. **5th and 6th rows:** Patt. Rep 1st to 4th rows once more. **Shape armhole. 1st row:** Cast off 7(9–9–11) sts, patt to end. **2nd row:** Patt. **3rd row:** Dec 1 st, patt to last 2 sts, dec 1 st. **4th row:** Patt. **5th row:** Dec 1 st, patt to end. **6th and 7th rows:** As 5th row. **8th row:** Patt. Rep 3rd to 8th rows once(once–twice–twice) more. **Sizes 34″/36″ and 38″/40″ only.** Rep 3rd to 5th rows once more. Keeping armhole edge straight [for all sizes] cont to dec for front on next and every foll 3rd row until 28(28–29–29) sts rem. Patt 3(3–2–2) rows, ending at armhole edge. **Shape shoulder.** Cast off 5(5–5–5) sts at beg of next row and 6(6–6–6) sts at beg of foll 3 alt rows. Patt 1 row. Cast off 5(5–6–6) rem sts.

Classic cable cardigan

RIGHT FRONT: With No 10 needles cast on 70(74-78-82) sts. **1st row:** P 2, * k 1, p 1; rep from * to end. **2nd row:** * K 1, p 1; rep from * to last 2 sts, k 2. Rep 1st and 2nd rows once more, then 1st row once. **Next row:** P 4(8-4-8) sts, * k 2 tog, k 1, p 5; rep from * to last 2 sts, k 2. Change to No 7 needles and patt. **1st row:** * P 2, sl 1 p-wise with wool at back of st, k 4; rep from * to last 6(10-6-10) sts, p 2, k 4(8-4-8). Complete to match Left Front, reversing all shapings and working one more row before commencing to shape front.

BACK: With No 10 needles cast on 139(147-155-163) sts. **1st row:** * P 1, k 1; rep from * to last st, p 1. **2nd row:** * K 1, p 1; rep from * to last st, k 1. Rep 1st and 2nd rows once more, then 1st row once. **Next row:** P 4(8-4-8) sts, * k 2 tog, k 1, p 5; rep from * to last 7(11-7-11) sts, k 2 tog, k 1, p 4(8-4-8). [122(130-136-144) sts] Change to No 7 needles and patt. **1st row:** K 4(8-4-8) sts, p 2, * sl 1 p-wise with wool at back of st, k 4, p 2; rep from * to last 4(8-4-8) sts, k 4(8-4-8). This sets patt. Cont in patt until Back measures same as Fronts to beg of armhole shaping, ending with a wrong side row. **Shape armholes.** Cast off 7(9-9-11) sts at beg of next 2 rows. Dec 1 st at beg of every row until 96(96-100-100) sts rem. Cont without shaping until armholes measure same as front armholes, ending with a wrong side row. **Shape shoulders.** Cast off 5(5-5-5) sts at beg of next 2 rows, and 6(6-6-6) sts at beg of foll 2 rows. **Shape back of neck.** **Next row:** Cast off 6(6-6-6) sts, patt 14(14-15-15) sts, including st already on needle, cast off 34(34-36-36) sts, patt to end. Cont on last set of sts as folls: **1st row:** Cast off 6(6-6-6) sts, patt to last 2 sts, dec 1 st. **2nd row:** Dec 1 st, patt to end. **3rd row:** As 1st. Work 1 row. Cast off 5(5-6-6) rem sts. Rejoin wool to rem sts at neck edge. **1st row:** Dec 1 st, patt to end. **2nd row:** Cast off 6(6-6-6) sts, patt to last 2 sts, dec 1 st. **3rd row:** As 1st. Cast off 5(5-6-6) rem sts.

SLEEVES: With No 10 needles cast on 47(47-51-51) sts. Work 5 rows in ribbing as given for Back. **Next row:** P 2(2-4-4) sts, * k into front and back of next st, p 5; rep from * to last 3(3-5-5) sts, k into front and back of next st, p 2(2-4-4). [55(55-59-59) sts]. Change to No 7 needles and patt. **1st row:** K 2(2-4-4) sts, * p 2, sl 1 p-wise with wool at back of st, k 4; rep from * to last 4(4-6-6) sts, p 2, k 2(2-4-4). This sets patt. Cont in patt, work 5 more rows. Keeping patt correct, inc 1 st at each end of next row, then every foll 6th row until there are 65(73-69-85) sts, and then 1 st at each end of every foll 8th row until there are 85(89-91-95) sts. Work until sleeve measures 18"(18½"-18½"-18½") from beg, ending with a wrong side row. **Shape top.** Cast off 7(9-9-11) sts at beg of next 2 rows. Dec 1 st at beg of every row until 45(45-45-45) sts rem. Cast off at beg of next and foll rows, 2 sts 4 times, 3 sts twice and 4 sts twice. Cast off 23 rem sts.

BORDER: With No 10 needles cast on 9 sts. **Next row:** K 1, * inc 1 st by picking up loop from between needles and p into back of it, k 1, p 1, inc 1 st by picking up loop from between needles and k into back of it, p 1, k 1; rep from * once more. [13 sts] Cont in rib. **1st row:** K 2, * p 1, k 1; rep from * to last st, k 1. **2nd row:** K 1, p 1; rep from * to last st, k 1. These two rows form rib. Cont in rib until border measures 3" from beg, ending with 2nd row. Make buttonhole in next 2 rows by casting off 3 centre sts in first row, and casting on 3 sts above those cast off in previous row. Work 26 rows. Make buttonhole in next 2 rows as before. Make four more buttonholes [six in all] with 26 rows between each. Work until border is long enough to fit along front and neck edges. Cast off firmly in rib.

TO MAKE UP: Join shoulder seams. Set in sleeves. Join side and sleeve seams using back st. Sew border to front and neck edges. Press seams. Sew on buttons to correspond with buttonholes.

Cardigans for beginners

Instructions are for a 34" bust. Changes for 36", 38" and 40" sizes are given in brackets.
MATERIALS: 17(18-19-20) ozs of Emu Scotch Double Knitting. One pair each Nos 9 and 11 needles. Ten buttons.

MEASUREMENTS: To fit a 34"(36"-38"-40") bust. Length to shoulder: 22½"(23"-24"-24½"), adjustable. Sleeve seam: 18"(18"-18½"-19"), adjustable.
TENSION: 6 sts and 8 rows to 1" over st-st on No 9 needles.

BACK: With No 11 needles cast on 109(115–121–127) sts. **Commence rib. 1st row:** K 1, * p 1, k 1; rep from * to end of row. **2nd row:** P 1, * k 1, p 1; rep from * to end of row. Rep these 2 rows 4 times more. Change to No 9 needles. Beg with a k row, cont in st-st until work measures 16″(16″–16½″–16½″) from beg, or required length to underarm ending with a p row. **Shape armholes. 1st row:** Cast off 5(5–6–6) sts, k to end. **2nd row:** Cast off 5(5–6–6) sts, p to end. **3rd row:** K 2 tog, k to last 2 sts, k 2 tog. **4th row:** P 2 tog, p to last 2 sts, p 2 tog. Rep 3rd and 4th rows twice more. **9th row:** K 2 tog, k to last 2 sts, k 2 tog. **10th row:** P to end. Rep 9th and 10th rows 1(2–2–3) times more. 83(87–91–95) sts. Work 20(22–26–28) rows without shaping on these sts. **Shape shoulders. 1st row:** Cast off 5 sts, k to end. **2nd row:** Cast off 5 sts, p to end. Rep 1st and 2nd shoulder shaping rows 4 times more. **11th row:** Cast off 4(6–7–8) sts, k to end. **12th row:** Cast off 4(6–7–8) sts, p to end. Cast off rem 25(25–27–29) sts.

LEFT FRONT: With No 11 needles cast on 55(57–61–63) sts. **Commence rib. 1st row:** K 1, * p 1, k 1; rep from * to end of row. **2nd row:** P 1, * k 1, p 1; rep from * to end of row. Rep these 2 rows 4 times more. Change to No 9 needles. Beg with a k row cont in st-st until work measures same as Back to underarm, ending with a p row. **Shape armhole. 1st row:** Cast off 5(5–6–6) sts, k to end. **2nd row:** P to end. **3rd row:** K 2 tog, k to end. **4th row:** P to last 2 sts, p 2 tog. Rep 3rd and 4th rows twice more. **9th row:** K 2 tog, k to end. **10th row:** P to end. Rep 9th and 10th rows 1(2–2–3) times more. 42(43–46–47) sts. Work 20(22–26–28) rows without shaping on these sts. **Shape shoulder. 1st row:** Cast off 5 sts, k to end. **2nd row:** P to end. Rep 1st and 2nd shoulder shaping rows once more. **5th row:** Cast off 5 sts, k to end. **Shape neck. 6th row:** Cast off 7(6–8–8) sts for neck, p to end. **7th row:** Cast off 5 sts, k to end. **8th row:** Cast off 3 sts, p to end. Rep 7th and 8th rows once more. Cast off rem 4(6–7–8) sts.

RIGHT FRONT: With No 11 needles cast on 55(57–61–63) sts. Work 10 rows rib as given for Left Front. Change to No 9 needles. Beg with a k row, cont in st-st until work measures same as Left Front to underarm, ending with a k row. **Shape armhole: 1st row:** Cast off 5(5–6–6) sts, p to end. **2nd row:** K to last 2 sts, k 2 tog. **3rd row:** P 2 tog, p to end. Rep 2nd and 3rd rows twice more. **8th row:** K to end. **9th row:** P 2 tog, p to end. Rep 8th and 9th rows 1(2–2–3) times more. 42(43–46–47) sts. Work 21(23–27–29) rows without shaping on these sts. **Shape shoulder. 1st row:** Cast off 5 sts, p to end. **2nd row:** K to end. Rep 1st and 2nd shoulder shaping rows once more. **5th row:** Cast off 5 sts, p to end. **Shape neck. 6th row:** Cast off 7(6–8–8) sts, k to end. **7th row:** Cast off 5 sts, p to end. **8th row:**

Cast off 3 sts, k to end. Rep 7th and 8th rows once more. Cast off rem 4(6–7–8) sts.

SLEEVES: [Make two] With No 11 needles cast on 45(47–51–53) sts. Work 10 rows rib as given for Left Front. Change to No 9 needles. Cont in st-st. **1st row:** K into front then into back of first st, k to last 2 sts, k into front then into back of next st, k 1. [2 sts increased] Beg with a p row, work 7 rows without shaping. Rep the last 8 rows until there are 75(79–85–89) sts. Cont in st-st without shaping until sleeve measures 18″(18″–18½″–19″) from beg, measured on the straight, or required length to underarm, ending with a p row. **Shape sleeve top. 1st row:** Cast off 5(5–6–6) sts, k to end. **2nd row:** Cast off 5(5–6–6) sts, p to end. **3rd row:** K 2 tog, k to last 2 sts, k 2 tog. **4th row:** P

61

Cardigans for beginners

to end. Rep 3rd and 4th rows until 39(39–41–41) sts rem, then rep 3rd row only once more. Mark each end of last row with coloured thread. **Commence saddle shoulder.** Beg with a p row work 1(3–1–3) rows without shaping. **Next row:** K 2 tog, k to last 2 sts, k 2 tog. Beg with a p row work 3 rows without shaping. Rep last 4 rows until 23 sts rem. **Next row:** K 2 tog, k to last 2 sts, k 2 tog. **Next row:** P to end. **Shape neck edge. 1st row:** K 6 sts, turn and leave rem sts on a holder for time being. **2nd row:** P 2 tog, p to end. **3rd row:** K 2 tog, k to end. **4th row:** P 2 tog, p to end. **5th row:** K to end. Rep 4th and 5th rows once more. **Next row:** P 2 sts. Cast off. With right side of work facing rejoin wool to inner edge of rem sts on holder, cast off next 9 sts, k rem 6 sts. **2nd row:** P to last 2 sts, p 2 tog. **3rd row:** K to last 2 sts, k 2 tog. **4th row:** P to last 2 sts, p 2 tog. **5th row:** K to end. Rep 4th and 5th rows once more. **Next row:** P 2 sts. Cast off.

TO MAKE UP: Press work very lightly on wrong side under a damp cloth with a warm iron. Use back st for seams except ribbed parts, where a woven flat seam is used. Starting from coloured thread markers, join side edges of sleeve saddle shoulders to shoulder edges of Back and Fronts. Join curve of sleeve top to curve of armhole. Join side and sleeve seams. **Neckband.** With right side of work facing and No 11 needles, join wool to neck edge of Right Front and k up 12(12–13–14) sts along curve of front neck, k up 25 sts around neck edge of saddle shoulder of right sleeve, k up 25(25–27–29) sts across back neck, k up 25 sts around neck edge of saddle shoulder of left sleeve and k up 12(12–13–14) sts along curve of left front neck. 99(99–103–107) sts. **1st row:** P 1, * k 1, p 1; rep from * to end of row. **2nd row:** K 1, * p 1, k 1; rep from * to end of row. Rep these 2 rows 3 times more, then 1st row once. Cast off in rib. **Button band.** With No 11 needles cast on 11 sts. **1st row:** K 1, * p 1, k 1; rep from * to end. **2nd row:** P 1, * k 1, p 1; rep from * to end. Rep these 2 rows until Band is long enough to fit along front edge when slightly stretched. Cast off in rib. Mark positions for ten buttons, first to come ½″ above cast on edge, and last to come ½″ below cast off edge with eight more evenly spaced between. **Buttonhole band:** Work as given for Button band, making buttonholes (when markers on Button band are reached) as follows: **1st buttonhole row:** Rib 4 sts, cast off 3 sts, rib 4 sts. **2nd buttonhole row:** Rib 4 sts, cast on 3 sts, rib 4 sts. Sew bands to front edges, joining Buttonhole band to Right Front for woman's Cardigan or to Left Front for man's Cardigan. Sew on buttons.

His and her moss stitch sweater

Instructions are for a 36″ bust. Changes for 38″, 40″, 42″ and 44″ sizes are given in brackets.

MATERIALS: 25(26–27–28–29) ozs Lister Lavenda Double Knitting wool. One pair each Nos 10 and 11 needles.

MEASUREMENTS: To fit a 36″(38″–40″–42″–44″) bust. Length at centre back: 25½″(26″–26″–26″–26″), adjustable. Sleeve seam: 18″(18½″–19″–19½″–20″), adjustable.

TENSION: 12½ sts and 17 rows to 2″ over moss-st on No 10 needles.

NOTE: Moss-st is worked by k 1, p 1 all along the row and on next and following rows k sts are knitted and p sts are purled.

BACK: With No 12 needles cast on 119(125–131–137–143) sts. **1st row:** (Right side) P 1, * k 1, p 1; rep from * to end of row. **2nd row:** K 1, * p 1, k 1; rep from * to end of row. Rep these 2 rows 9 times more, inc 1 st at each end of last row. 121(127–133–139–145) sts. Change to No 10 needles and moss-st. Cont in moss-st until work measures 17″ from beg, or required length to underarm ending with a wrong side row. **Shape armholes.** Cast off 1 st at beg of next 2 rows. ** **1st dec row:** K 3, k 2 tog, moss-st to last 5 sts, k 2 tog tbl, k 3. **2nd dec row:** P 4, moss-st to last 4 sts, p 4. **3rd dec row:** K 4, moss-st to last 4 sts, k 4. **4th dec row:** P 4, moss-st to last 4 sts, p 4. Rep 1st to 4th dec rows 12(12–13–13–14) times more, then 1st dec row once. 91(97–101–107–111) sts. Work 7(9–9–9–9) rows in moss-st working 4 sts at each end in st-st. **Shape shoulders. 1st row:** K 4, moss-st to last 4 sts, turn. **2nd row:** Sl 1 p-wise, p 3, moss-st to last 4 sts, turn. **3rd row:** Sl 1 k-wise, k 3, moss-st to last 8 sts, turn. **4th row:** Sl 1 p-wise, p 3, moss-st to last 8 sts, turn. Cont in this way working 4 sts less at end of every row until last 2 rows are worked as folls: Sl 1 k-wise, k 3, moss st to last 28(28–28–32–32) sts, turn. Sl 1 p-wise, p 3, moss-st to last 28(28–28–32–32) sts, turn. **Next row:** Sl 1 k-wise, k 3, moss-st to end. Work 3 more rows in moss-st across all sts.

Next row: Cast off 27(29–30–32–33) sts, moss-st 37 (39–41–43–45) sts, cast off rem 27(29–30–32–33) sts. Leave centre sts on holder for back neck.

FRONT: Work as for Back to **. Rep 1st to 4th dec rows as given for Back 13(13–14–14–15) times, ending with a 4th row. 93(99–103–109–113) sts. **Shape neck. Next row:** K 3, k 2 tog, moss-st 34(37–38–40–41) sts, turn. Complete left shoulder first. Keeping armhole edge straight, dec 1 st at neck edge on next 8 rows, then on foll alt rows 3(4–4–4–4) times. 27(29–30–32–33) sts. Work 3 rows in moss-st after last dec row. **Next row:** K 3, k up loop lying between sts, moss-st to end. Work 3 rows in moss-st. Rep last 4 rows once more, then first of these rows once more. 30(32–33–35–36) sts. Work 1 row. Cast off. Sl centre 15(15–17–19–21) sts on to a holder. With right side of work facing and No 10 needles, rejoin wool to rem 39(42–43–45–46) sts. Moss-st to last 5 sts, k 2 tog tbl, k 3. Complete to match left shoulder reversing shaping.

SLEEVES: With No 12 needles cast on 53(55–57–59–61) sts. Work 24 rows in rib as given for back inc 1 st at each end of last row. 55(57–59–61–63) sts. Change to No 10 needles and work in moss-st, inc 1 st at each end of 7th and every foll 6th row until there are 91(93–97–99–103) sts. Cont without shaping until sleeve measures 18″(18½″–19″–19½″–20″) from beg, or required length to underarm, ending with a wrong side row. **Shape top.** Cast off 1 st at beg of next 2 rows. **1st dec row:** K 3, k 2 tog, moss-st to last 5 sts, k 2 tog tbl, k 3. **2nd dec row:** P 4, moss-st to last 4 sts, p 4. **3rd dec row:** K 3, k 3 tog, moss-st to last 6 sts, k 3 tog tbl, k 3. **4th dec row:** P 4, moss-st to last 4 sts, p 4. Rep these 4 dec rows 10 times more, then 1st and 2nd rows 1(1–2–2–3) times more. 21(23–25–27–29) sts. Cast off 6(6–6–7–7) sts at beg of next 2 rows. Cast off rem 9(11–13–13–15) sts.

NECK RIBBING: With right side of work facing, sl sts from back neck holder on to No 12 needle.*** Beg with a 2nd rib row as given for Back work 8 rows in rib. **Next row:** K. Work 8 more rows in rib. Cast off in rib. *** With right side of Front facing and No 12 needles k up 31(31–32–31–31) sts down left side of neck, k up 1(k up 1–p 1, k up 1–k 1, p 1, k up 1–k up 1), * p 1, k 1, p 1, k up 1; rep from * 4(4–4–4–6) times more, then k up 31(k up 31–p 1, k up 32–p 1, k 1, k up 31–k up 31) up right side of neck. [83(83–87–87–91) sts.] Rep from *** to *** as given for back neck.

TO MAKE UP: Press each piece under a damp cloth with a hot iron. Join shoulder, side and sleeve seams using back st. Join neckband seams. Set in sleeves, the first inc st being shoulder line for centre of sleeve top. Press seams. Turn neck ribbing in half to wrong side and sl st. Press seams.

Fair Isle pullovers

Instructions are for a 32″ bust/chest. Changes for 34″, 36″, 38″, 40″, 42″ and 44″ sizes are given in brackets.

MATERIALS: Short version. 5(6–6–6–7–7–7) ozs Lee Target Motoravia 4-ply in main shade, A; 1(1–1–2–2–2–2) ozs in contrast, B; 1(1–1–1–2–2–2) ozs each in contrasts, C, D, E; 1(1–1–1–1–1–1) ozs in contrast, F. **Long version.** 6(6–7–7–8–8–8) ozs of same in main shade A; 2(2–2–2–2–2–2) ozs each of contrasts B and C; 1(1–1–1–2–2–2) ozs in contrast, D; 2(2–2–2–2–2–2) ozs in contrast, E; 1(1–1–1–1–1–1) ozs in contrast, F. One pair each Nos 10 and 12 needles. Set of four No 12 needles, pointed at both ends.

MEASUREMENTS: To fit a 32″(34″–36″–38″–40″–42″–44″) bust/chest. Length to shoulder: **Short version.** 17½″(18″–18½″–19″–19½″–20″–20½″); **Long version.** 22½″ (23″–23½″–24″–24½″–25″–25½″).

TENSION: 8 sts to 1″ on No 10 needles over Fair Isle pattern.

BACK: With No 12 needles and A, cast on 137(145–153–161–169–177–185) sts. **1st row:** K 1, * p 1, k 1; rep from * to end. **2nd row:** P 1, * k 1, p 1; rep from * to end. Rep these 2 rows for 4″, ending with a 2nd row. Change to No 10 needles. Join in B. **Commence Fair Isle pattern. 1st row:** K 1B, * 1A, 1B; rep from * to end. **2nd row:** P 1A, * 1B, 1A; rep from * to end. **3rd row:** As 1st. **4th row:** Join in C. P 1C, * 3A, 1C; rep from * to end. **5th row:** K 2C, * 1A, 3C; rep from * to last 3 sts, 1A, 2C. **6th row:** P 1C, * 1A, 5C, 1A, 1C; rep from * to end. **7th row:** K 1A, * 3C, 1A; rep from * to end. **8th row:** As 6th. **9th row:** As 5th. **10th row:** As 4th. **11th to 13th rows:** Join in B and work as 1st to 3rd rows. **14th row:** Join in D. P 1A, * 3D, 1A; rep from * to end. **15th row:** K 1A, * 2D, 3A, 2D, 1A; rep from * to end. **16th row:** P 1A, * 1D, 1A; rep from * to end. **17th row:** K 4A, * 1D, 7A; rep from * to last 5 sts, 1D, 4A. **18th row:** As 16th. **19th row:** As 15th. **20th row:** As 14th. **21st to 23rd rows.** Join in B and work as 1st to 3rd rows. **24th row:** Join in E and F. P 2F, * 2A, 1E, 2A, 3F; rep from * to last 7 sts, 2A, 1E, 2A, 2F. **25th row:** K 1F, * 1A, 2E, 1A, 2E, 1A, 1F; rep from * to end. **26th row:** P 1A, * 2E, 3A, 2E, 1A; rep from * to end. **27th row:** K as 26th row. **28th row:** P 1A, * 2E, 1A, 1F, 1A, 2E, 1A; rep from * to end. **29th row:** K as 28th row. **30th row:** P 1A, * 1E, 2F, 1A, 2F, 1E, 1A; rep from * to end. **31st row:** As 29th. **32nd row:** As 28th. **33rd row:** As 27th. **34th row:** As 26th. **35th row:** As 25th. **36th row:** As 24th. These 36 rows form patt and are rep throughout. Cont in patt until work measures 11″ from beg for Short version, or 16″ for Long version, ending with a p row. **Shape armholes.** Keeping patt correct, cast off at beg of next and every row 6(6–7–7–7–8–8) sts 4 times and 6(7–6–7–8–7–8) sts twice. 101(107–113–119–125–131–137) sts. Cont without shaping until armholes measure 6½″(7″–7½″–8″–8½″–9″–9½″) from beg, ending with a p row. **Shape shoulders.** Cast off at beg of next and every row 6(7–7–8–8–8–9) sts 8 times and 7(5–7–5–7–9–7) sts twice. Leave rem 39(41–43–45–47–49–51) sts on holder.

FRONT: Work as given for Back until Front measures 1½″ less than Back to underarm, ending with a p row. **Divide for neck. Next row:** Patt 68(72–76–80–84–88–92) sts, turn. Complete this side first. Dec 1 st at neck edge on 2nd and every foll 3rd row until work measures same as Back to underarm, ending with a p row. **Shape armholes.** Work as given for Back, **at the same time** cont to dec 1 st at neck edge on every foll 4th row until 31(33–35–37–39–41–43) sts rem. Cont without shaping until armhole measures same as Back to shoulder, ending with a p row. **Shape shoulder.** Cast off at beg of next and every foll alt row 6(7–7–8–8–8–9) sts 4 times and 7(5–7–5–7–9–7) sts once. With right side of work facing, rejoin wool to rem sts, sl first st on to holder and patt to end. Complete to match first side, reversing shaping.

NECKBAND: Join shoulder seams using back st. With right side of work facing and using set of four No 12 needles and A, k across sts on holder for back neck, k up 60(63–66–69–72–75–78) sts down front neck, k centre front st on holder and k up 60(63–66–69–72–75–78) sts up other side of front neck. 160(168–176–184–192–200–208) sts. Arrange sts on 3 needles. **Next round.** * K 1, p 1; rep from * to 2 sts before centre front st, p 2 tog, k 1, p 2 tog, rib to end. Rep this round for ¾″, working one st less on either side on centre front st. Cast off in rib, still dec at centre front.

ARMBANDS: With right side of work facing, No 12 needles and A, k up 18(19–20–21–22–23–24) sts along cast off sts at armhole, 48(51–54–57–60–63–66) sts up side of armhole to shoulder, 47(50–53–56–59–62–65) sts down side of armhole and 18(19–20–21–22–23–24) sts along other cast off sts. 131(139–147–155–163–171–179) sts. **1st row:** P 1, * k 1, p 1; rep from * to end. **2nd row:** Rib 16(17–18–19–20–21–22) sts, work 3 tog, rib to last 19(20–21–22–23–24–25) sts, work 3 tog, rib to end. **3rd row:** As 1st. **4th row:** Rib 15(16–17–18–19–20–21) sts, work 3 tog, rib to last 18(19–20–21–22–23–24) sts, work 3 tog, rib to end. Cont in this way, dec on every alt row until Band measures ¾″. Cast off in rib.

TO MAKE UP: Press work under a damp cloth with a warm iron. Join side seams using back st. Join armbands. Press seams.

Aran sampler cardigan

Instructions are for a 34"/36" bust. Changes for 38"/40" size are given in brackets.

MATERIALS: 15(16) 50 grm balls of Mahony's Blarney Bainin. One pair each Nos 7, 8 and 10 needles for first size and one pair each Nos 6, 7 and 9 needles for second size. Two cable needles. Seven (eight) buttons.

MEASUREMENTS: To fit a 34"/36"(38"/40") bust. Length: 24"(27"). Sleeve seam: 17"(19").

TENSION: 10 sts and 13 rows to 2" over st-st on No 7 needles. 9 sts and 11½ rows to 2" over st-st on No 6 needles.

ABBREVIATIONS: Cable 5: Sl next 2 sts on to cable needle and leave at front, sl next st on to 2nd cable needle and leave at back, k next 2 sts, then p 1 from back cable needle and k 2 from front cable needle. **C3R:** [Cross 3 to the right] Sl next st on to cable needle and leave at back, k 2, then p 1 from cable needle. **C3L:** [Cross 3 to the left] Sl next 2 sts on to cable needle and leave at front, p 1, then k 2 from cable needle. **T2P:** [Twist 2 p-wise] Put needle behind first st on left-hand needle, p the 2nd st, then p 1st st and sl both off. **T2R:** Miss 1st st on left-hand needle, k 2nd st, then p 1st st and sl both off. **T2L:** Put needle behind 1st st on left-hand needle, p 2nd st, then k 1st st and sl both off. **C4F:** [Cable 4 front] Sl next 2 sts on to cable needle at front, k 2, then k 2 from cable needle. **C4B:** As C4F but leave 2 sts at back on cable needle. **C2B:** Sl next st on to cable needle and hold at back, k 1 tbl, then p 1 from cable needle. **C2F:** Sl next st on to cable needle and hold at front, p 1, then k 1 tbl from cable needle.

BACK: With No 7(6) needles cast on 102(102) sts. K 1 row. Work in Bramble stitch. **1st row:** [Right side] P. **2nd row:** K 1, * [k 1, p 1, k 1] into next st – called 3 in to 1, p 3 tog; rep from * to last st, k 1. **3rd row:** P. **4th row:** K 1, * p 3 tog, 3 into 1; rep from * to last st, k 1. Rep these 4 rows 3 times more. Change to No 8(7) needles and k 4 rows [g-st]. Change to No 7(6) needles, and work in Diamond patt. **1st row:** P 9, * cable 5, p 11; rep from * ending last rep, p 8 instead of p 11. **2nd and every wrong side row:** K all sts purled in previous row and p all sts knitted in previous row. **3rd row:** P 8, * C3R, k 1, C3L, p 9; rep from * ending last rep, p 7. **5th row:** P 7, * C3R, k 1, p 1, k 1, C3L, p 7; rep from * ending last rep, p 6. **7th row:** P 6, * C3R, [k 1, p 1] twice, k 1, C3L, p 5; rep from * to end. **9th row:** P 5, * C3R, [k 1, p 1] 3 times, k 1, C3L, p 3; rep from * ending last rep, p 4. **11th row:** P 5, * C3L, [p 1, k 1] 3 times, p 1, C3R, p 3; rep from * ending last rep, p 4. **13th row:** P 6, * C3L, [p 1, k 1] twice, p 1, C3R, p 5; rep from * to end. **15th row:** P 7, * C3L, p 1, k 1, p 1, C3R, p 7; rep from * ending last rep, p 6. **17th row:** P 8, * C3L, p 1, C3R, p 9; rep from * ending last rep, p 7. **19th row:** As 1st row. **20th row:** As 2nd row. Change to No 8(7) needles and g-st 4 rows, but in 3rd row inc in 34th and 68th sts. 104(104) sts. Change to No 7(6) needles and work in Trellis patt. **1st row:** P 3, * k 2, p 4; rep from *, ending last rep, p 3. **2nd row:** K 3, * T2P, k 4; rep from *, ending last rep, k 3. **3rd row:** P 2, * T2R, T2L, p 2; rep from * to end. **4th row:** K 2, * p 1, k 2; rep from * to end. **5th row:** P 1, * T2R, p 2, T2L; rep from * to last st, p 1. **6th row:** K 1, p 1, k 4, * T2P, k 4; rep from * to last 2 sts, p 1, k 1. **7th row:** P 1, * T2L, p 2, T2R; rep from *, ending last rep, p 1. **8th row:** As 4th. **9th row:** P 2, * T2L, T2R, p 2; rep from * to end. **10th row:** As 2nd. Rep 3rd to 10th rows inclusive once more. Change to No 8(7) needles and g-st 4 rows, but in 3rd row k 2 tog on 35th and 36th, 69th and 70th sts. 102(102) sts. Change to No 7(6) needles and work Crossed Diamond patt. **1st row:** P 1, k 2, p 6, [C4F, p 6] 9 times, k 2, p 1. **2nd row:** K 1, p 2, [k 6, p 4] 9 times, k 6, p 2, k 1. **3rd row:** P 1, [C3L, p 4, C3R] 10 times, p 1. **4th and every wrong side row:** K all sts purled on previous row and p all knitted sts as in 2nd row. **5th row:** P 2, [C3L, p 2, C3R, p 2] 10 times. **7th row:** P 3, C3L, C3R, [p 4, C3L, C3R] 9 times, p 3. **9th row:** P 4, C4B, [p 6, C4B] 9 times, p 4. **11th row:** P 3, C3R, C3L, [p 4, C3R, C3L] 9 times, p 3. **13th row:** P 2, [C3R, p 2, C3L, p 2] 10 times. **15th row:** P 1, C3R, [p 4, C3L, C3R] 9 times, p 4, C3L, p 1. **16th row:** As 2nd row. **17th and 18th rows:** Rep 1st and 2nd rows. Change to No 8(7) needles and g-st 4 rows, dec 1 st in centre of 3rd row. 101(101) sts. Change to No 7(6) needles and work Zig-Zag patt. **1st row:** P 7, * [p 1, k 1 tbl] 3 times, p 6; rep from * ending last rep, p 4. **2nd row:** K 4, * [p 1, k 1] 3 times, k 6; rep from * ending last rep, p 7. **3rd row:** P 7, * [C2B] 3 times, p 6; rep from * ending last rep, p 4. **4th and every wrong side row:** K all sts purled in previous row and p all k sts as in 2nd row. **5th row:** P 6, * [C2B] 3 times, p 6; rep from * ending last rep, p 5. **7th row:** P 5, * [C2B] 3 times, p 6; rep from * ending last rep, p 6. **9th row:** P 4, * [C2B] 3 times, p 6; rep from * ending last rep, p 7. **11th row:** P 4, * [C2F] 3 times, p 6; rep from * ending last rep, p 7. **13th row:** P 5, * [C2F] 3 times, p 6; rep from *

Aran sampler cardigan

to ending. **15th row:** P 6, * [C2F] 3 times, p 6; rep from * ending last rep, p 5. **17th row:** P 7, * [C2F] 3 times, p 6; rep from * ending last rep, p 4. **18th row:** As 2nd row. Change to No 8(7) needles and g-st 4 rows, inc 10 times evenly across 3rd row. 111(111) sts. Change to No 7(6) needles and work Cable and Moss st patt. **1st row:** P 2, * k 4, p 1, k 4, [p 1, k 1] twice, p 1; rep from * to last 11 sts, k 4, p 1, k 4, p 2. **2nd row:** K 2, * p 4, k 1, p 4, k 2, p 1, k 2; rep from * to last 11 sts, p 4, k 1, p 4, k 2. **3rd row:** P 2, * C4B, p 1, C4F, [p 1, k 1] twice, p 1; rep from * to last 11 sts, C4B, p 1, C4F, p 2. **4th row:** As 2nd. **5th and 6th rows:** Rep 1st and 2nd rows. **7th row:** P 2, * C4F, p 1, C4B, [p 1, k 1] twice, p 1; rep from * to last 11 sts, C4F, p 1, C4B, p 2. **8th row:** As 2nd row. These eight rows form patt. **Shape armholes.** Cont in patt, cast off 6 sts at beg of next 2 rows, dec 1 st at each end of next 5 right-side rows. Work 1 row patt. 89(89) sts. Change to No 8(7) needles. **Next row:** K 2 tog, k 6, [k 2 tog, k 10] 6 times, k 2 tog, k 5, k 2 tog 80(80) sts. Work 3 rows g-st. Change to No 7(6) needles and work Tree of Life patt. **1st row:** P 1, * p 4, C2B, k 1 tbl, C2F, p 4; rep from * to last st, p 1. **2nd row:** K 1, * k 4, [p 1 tbl, k 1] twice, p 1 tbl, k 4; rep from * to last st, k 1. **3rd row:** P 1, * p 3, C2B, p 1, k 1 tbl, p 1, C2F, p 3; rep from * to last st, p 1. **4th row:** K 1, * k 3, p 1 tbl, [k 2, p 1 tbl] twice, k 3; rep from * to last st, k 1. **5th row:** P 1, * p 2, C2B, p 2, k 1 tbl, p 2, C2F, p 2; rep from * to last st, p 1. **6th row:** K 1, * k 2, p 1 tbl, [k 3, p 1 tbl] twice, k 2; rep from * to last st, k 1. **7th row:** P 1, * p 1, C2B, p 3, k 1 tbl, p 3, C2F, p 1; rep from * to last st, p 1. **8th row:** K 1, * k 1, p 1 tbl, [k 4, p 1 tbl] twice, k 1; rep from * to last st, k 1. Rep these eight rows once more. Change to No 8(7) needles and g-st 4 rows, inc twice in 3rd row. 82(82) sts. Change to No 7(6) needles and work in Open Cable patt. **1st row:** P 1, * p 2, k 1 tbl; rep from * to last 3 sts, p 3. **2nd row:** K 1, * k 2, p 1 tbl; rep from * to last 3 sts, k 3. **3rd row:** P 1, * p 2, C2F, C2B; rep from * to last 3 sts, p 3. **4th row:** K 4, * p 2 tbl, k 4; rep from * to end. **5th row:** P 4, * sl next st on to cable needle and hold at front, k 1 tbl, then k 1 tbl from cable needle, p 4; rep from * to end. **6th row:** As 4th. **7th row:** P 1, * p 2, C2B, C2F; rep from * to last 3 sts, p 3. **8th row:** As 2nd. **9th and 10th rows:** Rep 1st and 2nd rows. **11th to 18th rows:** Rep 1st to 8th rows inclusive. Change to No 8(7) needles and g-st 4 rows. **Shape shoulders.** Cont in g-st, cast off 6 sts at beg of next 4 rows and 7 sts at beg of foll 4 rows. Cast off rem 30 sts.

LEFT FRONT: With No 7(6) needles cast on 50(50) sts. K 1 row. Work in Bramble stitch as for Back. Change to No 8(7) needles and work 4 rows g-st. Change to No 7(6) needles and work Diamond patt as for Back but with one p st less at each end and one less between diamonds thus: **1st row:** P 8, * cable 5, p 10; rep from * ending last rep, p 7. **3rd row:** P 7, * C3R, k 1, C3L, p 8; rep from * ending last rep, p 6. Cont in patt as set until 20 rows are complete Change to No 8(7) needles and g-st 4 rows. Change to No 7(6) needles and work Trellis patt as given for Back. Change to No 8(7) needles and g-st 2 rows. **Next row:** [K 16, k twice into next st] twice, k 16. K one more row on 52 sts. Change to No 7(6) needles and work in Crossed Diamond patt as given for Back, reading 4 times for 9 times and 5 times for 10 times. Change to No 8(7) needles and g-st 4 rows, dec 1 st in centre of 3rd row. Change to No 7(6) needles and work in Zig-Zag patt as given for Back but with one p st less at each end thus; **1st row:** P 6, * [p 1, k 1 tbl] 3 times, p 6; rep from * ending last rep, p 3. **2nd row:** K 3, * [p 1, k 1] 3 times, k 6; rep from * to end. **3rd row:** P 6, * [C2B] 3 times, p 6; rep from * ending last rep, p 3. Cont in patt as set until 18 rows are complete. Change to No 8(7) needles and g-st 4 rows, inc 4 times evenly across 3rd row. 55(55) sts. Change to No 7(6) needles and work 8 rows Cable and Moss-St patt as given for Back. **Shape armholes.** Cont in patt, cast off 6 sts at beg of next row. Dec 1 st at armhole edge on next 5 right-side rows. Work 1 more row patt on 44 sts. Change to No 8(7) needles. **Next row:** K 2 tog [last armhole dec], [k 12, k 2 tog] twice, k 14. K 3 more rows on 41 sts. Change to No 7(6) needles and work Tree of Life patt as given for Back. Change to No 8(7) needles and g-st 4 rows, dec 1 st in centre of 3rd row. Change to No 7(6) needles and work Open Cable patt as given for Back on 5 rows. **Shape neck.** Keeping patt correct, cast off 7 sts at beg of next row, then dec 1 st at same edge on next 7 rows. Work 5 rows without shaping on 26 sts to complete patt. Change to No 8(7) needles and g-st 4 rows. **Shape shoulder.** Cont in g-st cast off at beg of armhole edge rows, 6 sts twice and 7 sts twice.

RIGHT FRONT: Work as for Left Front reversing armhole by working 1 extra row in patt before casting off 6 sts and reversing last armhole dec row by reading it backwards. Work 1 extra row also before shaping neck and shoulders.

SLEEVES: With No 10(9) needles cast on 46(46) sts. Work 2½″ in k 1, p 1 rib. Change to No 7(6) needles and patt. **1st row:** P 1, * k 8, p 1; rep from * to end. **2nd row:** K 1, * p 8, k 1; rep from * to end. **3rd and 4th rows:** Rep 1st and 2nd rows. **5th row:** P. **6th row:** K. These six rows form patt. Cont in patt inc 1 st at each end of foll 3rd and every foll 10th row until there are 62(62) sts, working inc sts into patt. Cont without shaping until sleeve measures 17″(19″) from beg, ending with a wrong side row. **Shape top.** Cast off 5 sts at beg of next 2 rows. Dec 1 st at each end of every right-side row until 30 sts rem, ending with a dec row, then each end of next 5 rows. Cast off 3 sts at beg of next 2 rows. Cast off rem 14 sts.

BORDERS AND NECK BAND: Join shoulder seams using back st. Mark front edge with pins as buttonhole guide, approx 3″(3¼″) from neck edge and 6 rows from lower edge, with 4(5) more evenly spaced between. With No 10(9) needles cast on 10 sts for Left Front border and work in p 1, k 1, rib [regarding 1st row as right side]. For Man's version only make buttonholes in this border as markers are reached thus: **Button-hole row:** [Right side facing] Rib 3, cast off 3, rib to end. **Next row:** Cast on 3 sts above those cast off in previous row. Work in rib until border fits front edge, slightly stretched, ending with a wrong side row. * Break wool and leave sts on a holder. Work Right Front border to match, working in k 1, p 1 rib and make buttonholes for Woman's version thus: **Buttonhole row:** Rib 4, cast off 3, rib to end. **Next row:** Cast on 3 sts above those cast off in previous row. Work as for Left Front border to *. Do not break wool but keep rib sts on same needle, k up 73 sts around neck and rib 10 sts from holder. Work 9 rows in k 1, p 1 rib [beg and end first row with p 1] making final buttonhole in 4th row as before. Cast off in rib.

TO MAKE UP: Pin out and press work on wrong side with a damp cloth and hot iron. Join side and sleeve seams using back st. Set in sleeves. Sew on front borders and buttons. Press seams.

Smock

Instructions are for a 32″/34″ bust. Changes for 34″/36″ and 36″/38″ sizes are given in brackets.

MATERIALS: 23(24–25) ozs of Sirdar Double Knitting. One pair each Nos 8 and 9 needles. Five small buttons.

MEASUREMENTS: Length: 30″(30″–30″). Sleeve seam: 19″(19″–19″).

TENSION: 5½ sts and 7½ rows to 1″ over st-st No 9's.

ABBREVIATIONS: C2F [Cross 2 front]—Take the needle in front of the first stitch on left-hand needle and knit the 2nd stitch; now knit the first stitch, slip both stitches off the needle together; g-st: [garter stitch]—Every row k.

FRONT: ** With No 9 needles cast on 122(130–138) sts. Work 17 rows g-st. Change to No 8 needles and st-st. Work until front measures 21″ from beg, ending with a p row. ** Change to No 9 needles. **Beg yoke patt and divide for front opening. 1st row:** [P 2, take

Smock

the needle in front of the first st on left-hand needle and k the 2nd st, k the first st, sl both sts off needle tog – called C2F –] 14(15–16) times, p 2, turn and cast on 6 sts for underflap, leaving rem sts on holder. **2nd row:** K 8, * p 2, k 2; rep from * to end. **3rd row:** [P 2, C2F] 14(15–16) times, p 2, k 6. **4th row:** As 2nd. 3rd and 4th rows form patt. Work 4 more rows. **Shape armhole.** Cast off 4(6–6) sts at beg of next row and 2(2–2) sts at beg of foll alt row. Dec 1 st at beg of every alt row until 52(52–56) sts rem. Work 26(22–22) rows without shaping, ending at opening edge. **Shape neck. Next row:** Work 12(12–12) sts and sl on to holder, patt to end. Work back to neck edge. Keeping armhole edge straight, dec 1 st at neck edge on next 7 rows and on foll 4(4–5) alt rows, ending at armhole edge. **Shape shoulder.** Dec 1 st at neck edge on alt rows twice more, cast off 6(6–8) sts at beg of next row and 7(7–7) sts at beg of foll 2 alt rows. Work 1 row. Cast off 7(7–8) sts rem. Sl sts from holder back on to needle. **1st row:** K 6, * p 2, C2F; rep from * to last 2 sts, p 2. **2nd row:** * K 2, p 2; rep from * to last 8 sts, k 8. Cont in patt. Work 4 more rows. **Next row:** [Make buttonhole] K 2, k 2 tog, w fwd, patt to end. Now making a buttonhole on every 12th row in this way, cont as follows: Work 2 more rows. **Shape armhole.** Cast off 4(6–6) sts at beg of next row and 2(2–2) sts at beg of foll alt row. Dec 1 st at beg of every alt row until 52(52–56) sts rem. Work 26(22–22) rows without shaping, ending at opening edge. **Shape neck. Next row:** K 6, p 2 tog, C2F, p 2 tog, sl these 10 sts on to a holder, patt to end. Keeping armhole edge straight, dec 1 st at neck edge on next 7 rows, then on foll 4(4–5) alt rows. Work 1 row, ending at armhole edge. Shape shoulder and complete neck shaping to match first side.

BACK: Work as given for Front from ** to **. Change to No 9 needles and beg yoke patt. **1st row:** * P 2, C2F; rep from * to last 2 sts, p 2. **2nd row:** * K 2, p 2; rep from * to last 2 sts, k 2. These two rows form patt. Work 6 more rows. **Shape armholes.** Cast off 4(6–6) sts at beg of next 2 rows and 2(2–2) sts at beg of foll 2 rows. Dec 1 st at beg of every row until 98(98–106) sts rem. Cont until armholes measure same as front to beg of shoulder shaping, ending with a wrong side row. **Shape shoulders.** Cast off 6(6–8) sts at beg of next 2 rows. **Shape back of neck. Next row:** Cast off 7(7–7) sts, patt 17(17–18) sts including st already on needle, cast off 38(38–40) sts, patt to end. Cont on last set of sts as follows: **1st row:** Cast off 7(7–7) sts to last 2 sts, dec 1 st. **2nd row:** Dec 1 st, patt to end. **3rd row:** As 1st. Work 1 row. Cast off 7(7–8) rem sts. Rejoin wool to rem sts at neck edge. **1st row:** Dec 1 st, patt to end. **2nd row:** Cast off 7(7–7) sts, work to last 2 sts, dec 1 st. **3rd row:** As 1st. Cast off rem 7(7–8) sts.

SLEEVES: With No 9 needles cast on 46(50–50) sts. **1st row:** * P 2, C2F; rep from * to last 2 sts, p 2. **2nd row:** * K 2, p 2; rep from * to last 2 sts, k 2. Rep 1st and 2nd rows for 3″, ending with 2nd row. Change to No 8 needles and st-st. Work 8 rows. Inc 1 st at each end of next row and then every 8th row until there are 58(62–62) sts, then 1 st at each end of every 10th row until there are 68(72–74) sts. Work until sleeve measures 19″(19″–19″) from beg, ending with a p row. **Shape top.** Cast off 4(6–6) sts at beg of next 2 rows, and 2(2–2) sts at beg of foll 2 rows. Dec 1 st at beg of every row until 32(32–32) sts rem. Cast off 2 sts at beg of next 4 rows, 3 sts at beg of foll 2 rows. Cast off rem 18 sts.

COLLAR: With No 9 needles cast on 33 sts. Work in g-st [1st row wrong side] until collar measures 14″ (14″–14½″) unstretched, ending with a right side row. Cast off k-wise.

POCKETS: [Make two] With No 9 needles cast on 33 sts. Work 17 rows g-st. Change to No 8 needles and st-st. Work until pocket measures 6″ from beg, ending with a p row. Cast off.

NECK BORDER: Press each piece lightly with warm iron and damp cloth. Join shoulder seams. Sl 10 sts on holder at right side of neck on to a No 9 needle, pick up and k 16(16–17) sts up right side of neck, 37(37–39) sts along back neck edge, [pick up 1 st only from each p rib] and 16(16–17) sts down left side of neck. Work across the 12 sts on holder as follows: P 2 tog, C2F, p 2 tog, k 6. Cont in g-st. Work 5 rows. Make buttonhole in next row as before. Work 4 rows. Cast off firmly k-wise.

TO MAKE UP: Sew sleeves into armholes. Join side and sleeve seams. Sew lower edge of underflap neatly at back of overflap. Sew pockets to front as illustrated; sew side edge of collar to cast-off edge of neck border, starting and ending ½″ from centre front edges. Press seams. Sew on buttons to correspond with buttonholes.

Ribbed hat

MATERIALS: 3 balls Patons Doublet. One pair No 5 needles. Cotton wool for stuffing.
TENSION: 4½ sts to 1″ over st-st on No 5 needles. With No 5 needles cast on 94 sts. **1st row:** * P 2, k 2; rep from * to last 2 sts, p 2. **2nd row:** * K 2, p 2; rep from * to last 2 sts, k 2. Rep these 2 rows for 6½″ ending with a 2nd row. Cont in st-st. Beg with a k row work 8 rows. **Next row:** K 4, * k 2 tog, k 4; rep from * to end. [79 sts] Work 5 rows st-st. **Next row:** K 1, * k 2 tog, k 3; rep from * to last 3 sts, k 2 tog, k 1. [63 sts] Work 5 rows st-st. **Next row:** K 3, * k 2 tog, k 2; rep from * to end. [48 sts] Work 3 rows st-st. **Next row:** K 2, * k 2 tog, k 1; rep from * to last 4 sts, k 2 tog, k 2. [33 sts] Work 3 rows st-st. **Next row:** K 1, * k 2 tog; rep from * to end. [17 sts] **Next row:** P 1, * p 2 tog; rep from * to end. [9 sts] Break wool leaving enough to thread through sts, draw up and fasten off.

TO MAKE UP: Join seam, reversing the seam for the ribbing. Press lightly. Form cotton wool into a roll 24″ long and about 2″ in diameter. Place roll of cotton wool round hat in centre of the ribbing. Fold ribbing over roll and oversew the cast-on edge neatly to the last row of ribbing.

Angora cardigans

Instructions are for a 32″ bust. Changes for 34″, 36″ and 38″ sizes are given in brackets.
MATERIALS: 14(15–16–17) ½-oz balls of Patons Fuzzy-Wuzzy. One pair each Nos 10 and 12 needles. Seven buttons if required.
MEASUREMENTS: To fit a 32″(34″–36″–38″) bust. Length: 23½″(23½″–24½″–24½″), adjustable. Sleeve seam: 12½″(12½″–12½″–12½″).
TENSION: 7 sts and 9 rows to 1″ on No 10 needles.
LEFT FRONT: Pocket lining. With No 10 needles, cast on 33(33–35–35) sts. Work 37(37–39–39) rows in st-st, ending with a k row. Break yarn and leave sts on spare needle. With No 12 needles cast on 67(71–75–79) sts. Change to No 10 needles. **1st row:** [Wrong side] Sl 1, * p 1, k 1; rep from * to end. **2nd row:** K 2, * p 1, k 1; rep from * to last st, k 1. Rep 1st and 2nd rows 5 times more, then 1st row once. **Next row:** K to last 11 sts, rib 11 sts for border. [Always k border sts firmly, or use a size finer needle for the border sts only.] **Next row:** Sl 1, [p 1, k 1] 5 times, p to end. Cont in st-st with 11 sts in rib for border. Work 34(34–36–36) more rows. Work pocket in next 2 rows as folls: **Next row:** K 42(44–47–49) sts, sl last 33(33–35–35) sts just worked on to a st holder, patt to end. **Next row:** Work to end, working pocket lining sts in place of those sts on a holder. Cont until front measures 14½″(14½″–15″–15″) from beg, or required length to underarm, ending at side edge. **Shape armhole. Next row:** Cast off 12(15–18–20) sts, patt to end. Work until armhole measures 6″(6″–6¼″–6¼″), ending at centre front edge. **Shape neck. Next row:** Work 17(17–17–18) sts and sl on to a holder, patt to end. Work back to neck edge. Keeping armhole edge straight, dec 1 st at neck edge on the next 9 rows, then on the foll 6 alt rows, ending at armhole edge.

Angora cardigans

Shape shoulders. Dec at neck edge on alt rows twice more, cast off 6(5–6–6) sts at beg of next row and 5(6–6–6) sts at beg of foll 2 alt rows. Work 1 row. Cast off 5(5–5–6) rem sts. **Pocket border.** Sl sts from holder on to a No 12 needle. **Next row:** [Wrong side] [Sizes 32″ and 34″ only] * [K 1, p 1] twice, inc 1 st by picking up loop from between needles and k into back ·of it, p 1; rep from * to last 3 sts, k 1, p 1, k 1. **Next row:** [Wrong side] [Sizes 36″ and 38″ only] * [K 1, p 1] twice, k 1, inc 1 st by picking up loop from between needles and p into back of it; rep from * to last 5 sts, [k 1, p 1] twice, k 1. Cont in rib. **1st row:** K 2, * p 1, k 1; rep from * to last st, k 1. **2nd row:** * K 1, p 1; rep from * to last st, k 1. Rep first and 2nd rows 4 times more. Cast off in rib.

RIGHT FRONT: [Omit buttonholes if not required] Work pocket lining as for Left Front. With No 12 needles cast on 67(71–75–79) sts. Change to No 10 needles. **1st row:** [Wrong side] * K 1, p 1; rep from * to last st, k 1. **2nd row:** Sl 1, * k 1, p 1; rep from * to last 2 sts, k 2. Rep 1st and 2nd rows once more, then 1st row once. Make buttonhole in next 2 rows as folls: **Next row:** Rib 5, cast off 3, rib to end. **Next row:** Rib to end, casting on 3 sts over those cast off in preceeding row. Pin positions of 6 buttons on Left Front border, [7th will come in neck border], the bottom button level with buttonhole just worked, and the rest equally spaced. Note that as 7th buttonhole comes in neck border, the measurement between the top button and beg of neck shaping should be ½″ less than the measurement between the other buttons. Making buttonholes to correspond with marked positions, cont as folls: Work 6 more rows in rib. **Next row:** Rib 11 sts for border, k to end. **Next row:** P to last 11 sts, rib 11. Cont in st-st with 11 sts in rib for border, work 34 (34–36–36) more rows. Work pocket in next 2 rows as folls: **Next row:** Work 58(60–63–65) sts, sl last 33 (33–35–35) sts just worked on to a holder, k to end. **Next row:** Patt to end, working pocket lining sts in place of those on a holder. Cont until front measures 14½″(14½″–15″–15″) from beg, or required length to underarm, ending at side edge. [Work 1 more row than on Left Front] **Shape armhole. Next row:** Cast off 12(15–18–20) sts, patt to end. Cont until armhole measures 6″(6″–6¼″–6¼″), ending at centre front edge. **Shape neck. Next row:** Work 17(17–17–18) sts, sl these sts on to a holder, patt to end. Keeping armhole edge straight, dec 1 st at neck edge on next 9 rows and then on foll 6 alt rows. Work 1 row ending at armhole edge. Shape shoulder and complete neck shaping to

match Left Front. **Pocket border.** Work as for Left Front.

BACK: With No 12 needles cast on 119(127–135–143) sts. Change to No 10 needles. **1st row:** [Wrong side] * K 1, p 1; rep from * to last st, k 1. **2nd row:** K 2, * p 1, k 1; rep from * to last st, k 1. Rep 1st and 2nd rows 5 times more, then 1st row once. Cont in st-st. Work until back measures same as Fronts to underarm, ending with a p row. **Shape armholes.** Cast off 12(15–18–20) sts at beg of next 2 rows. Work until armholes measure same as fronts to beg of shoulder shaping, ending with a p row. **Shape shoulder.** Cast off 6(5–6–6) sts at beg of next 2 rows. **Shape back of neck. Next row:** Cast off 5(6–6–6) sts, k 13(14–14–15) sts including st already on the needle, cast off 47(47–47–49) sts, k to end. Cont on last set of sts as folls: **1st row:** Cast off 5(6–6–6) sts, p to last 2 sts, p 2 tog. **2nd row:** K 2 tog, k to end. **3rd row:** As 1st. Work 1 row. Cast off 5(5–5–6) rem sts. Rejoin yarn to rem sts at neck edge. **1st row:** P 2 tog, p to end. **2nd row:** Cast off 5(6–6–6) sts, k to last 2 sts, k 2 tog. **3rd row:** As 1st row. Cast off 5(5–5–6) rem sts.

SLEEVES: With No 12 needles cast on 83(83–87–87) sts. Change to No 10 needles. Work 13 rows in ribbing as given for back. Cont in st-st. Work until sleeve measures 9½″(9½″–9½″–9½″) from beg, ending with a p row. Inc one st at each end of next row, then every alt row until there are 99(99–103–103) sts, then one st at each end of every row until there are 121(121–125–125) sts. Work 17(20–24–27) rows without shaping. Cast off.

NECK BORDER: Press each piece lightly with warm iron and damp cloth. Join both shoulder seams. Sl 17(17–17–18) sts on holder at right neck edge, on to a No 12 needle. Pick up and k 31 sts up right neck edge, 57(57–57–59) sts along back neck edge and 31 sts down left neck edge, then work across sts on holder. **1st row:** Sl 1, * p 1, k 1; rep from * to end. **2nd row:** Sl 1, * k 1, p 1; rep from * to last 2 sts, k 2. Rep 1st and 2nd rows once more, then 1st row once. Make buttonhole in next 2 rows as given for Right Front. Work 6 more rows in rib. Cast off firmly in rib.

TO MAKE UP: Join side seams using back st. Join sleeve seams, reversing the seam for 6½″ from cuff edge, and leaving the straight edges at top open. Set in sleeves, sewing the straight edges at top of sleeves to the cast-off sts at underarms. Sew neatly round pocket linings on the wrong side. Sew side edges of pocket borders to fronts. Press seams lightly. Sew on buttons if required. Roll up cuffs.

Cap-sleeved sweaters

Relief stitch sweater

Instructions are for a 32″ bust. Changes for 34″ and 36″ sizes are given in brackets.

MATERIALS: 4(5–5) balls of Patons Cameo Crepe in main shade, A; 2(2–2) balls of same in contrast, B. One pair each Nos 10 and 12 needles. Set of four No 12 needles pointed at both ends.

MEASUREMENTS: Length: 19″.

TENSION: 7 sts and 9 rows to 1″.

FRONT: ** With No 10 needles and A cast on 4 sts. **1st row:** [Wrong side] P. **2nd row:** Inc in first st, [with the right-hand needle pick up p loop in previous row at back of next st to be knitted and k into it, k st on needle—called M1R] twice, inc in last st. **3rd row:** Inc in first st, p to last st, inc in last st. **4th row:** Inc in first st, k 3, [M1R] twice, k 3, inc in last st. **5th row:** As 3rd row. **6th row:** Inc in first st, k 6, [M1R] twice, k 6, inc in last st. **7th row:** As 3rd. **8th row:** Inc in first st, k 9, [M1R] twice, k 9, inc in last st. Cont in st-st inc in this way until there are 100(112–118) sts. Working in patt of 6 rows reverse st-st [p 1 row, k 1 row] 6 rows st-st, 6 rows reverse st-st and 22 rows st-st cont thus: P 2 centre sts on wrong side throughout cont inc as before until there are 128(140–146) sts. Work 1 row. **Next row:** K2 tog, work 61(67–70) sts, [M1R] twice, work to last 2 sts, k 2 tog. **Next row:** Patt to end. Rep last 2 rows 27 times more **. **Shape armholes and neck. Next row:** K 2 tog, patt 60(66–69) sts, k 2 tog, turn leaving rem sts on spare needle. Cont on these rem sts. Dec 1 st at each end of next 4 rows, then dec 1 st at neck edge on foll 3 rows. Work 27(27–29) rows without shaping, ending at neck edge. **Shape shoulder.** Keeping armhole edge straight, cast off at beg of next and alternate rows 3 sts 4 times and 4(5–5) sts 3 times. Work 1 row. Cast off 27(30–33) rem sts. Rejoin wool to rem sts at neck edge. **Next row:** K 2 tog, patt to last 2 sts, k 2 tog. Dec 1 st at each end of next 4 rows and dec at neck edge only on 3 foll rows. Work 26(26–28) rows without shaping, ending at neck edge. Shape shoulder to match first side.

BACK: Work as for front from ** to **. **Shape armholes.** Cont to inc in centre of work, dec 1 st at each end of next 5 rows. Work 9(9–11) rows, still inc in centre of work. **Shape neck. Next row:** Work 64(70–74) sts, k 2 tog turn, leaving rem sts on holder. Cont on these sts. Keeping armhole edge straight, dec 1 st at neck edge on next 14(14–15) rows. Work 6(6–5) rows without shaping, ending at neck edge. Shape shoulder as for front. Rejoin wool to rem sts at neck edge, k 2 tog, work to end. Keeping armhole edge straight, dec 1 st at neck edge on next 14(14–15) rows. Work 5(4–4) rows without shaping, ending at neck edge. Shape shoulder

to match first side.

FRONT WELT: With No 12 needles and B and with right side of work facing, k up 86(94–98) sts evenly along lower edge. Work 5 inches k 1, p 1 rib. Cast off loosely in rib.

BACK WELT: Work as for Front Welt.

NECK BORDER: Press each piece lightly with warm iron and damp cloth. Join shoulder seams. With set of four No 12 needles and B, k up 50 sts evenly along back neck edge, and 68(68–72) sts along Front neck edge. Work 10 rounds k 1, p 1 rib. Cast off loosely in rib.

ARMHOLE BORDERS: With No 12 needles and B, k up 92(92–96) sts round armhole edge. Work 5 rows k 1, p 1 rib. Cast off in rib.

TO MAKE UP: Join side seams including armhole borders. Press seams.

Striped sweater

Instructions are for a 34″ bust. Changes for 36″ and 38″ sizes are given in brackets.

MATERIALS: 2(2–2) balls of Patons Cameo Crepe in main shade, A; 3(3–4) balls of same in contrast, B; 1(1–1) ball of same in 2nd contrast, C. One pair each Nos 9 and 11 needles. Set of four No 11 double-pointed needles.

Measurements: Length: 17″.

TENSION: 6½″ sts and 8½ rows to 1″.

FRONT: ** With No 9 needles and A, cast on 4 sts. **1st row:** [Wrong side] P. **2nd row:** Inc in first st, [with the right hand needle pick up the p loop in previous row at back of next st and k into it, k next st on needle—called M1R] twice, inc in last st. **3rd row:** Inc in first st, p to last st, inc in last st. **4th row:** Inc in first st, k 3, [M1R] twice, k 3, inc in last st. **5th row:** As 3rd row. **6th row:** Inc in first st, k 6, [M1R] twice, k 6, inc in last st. **7th row:** As 3rd. **8th row:** Inc in first st, k 9, [M1R] twice, k 9, inc in last st. Cont in st-st inc in this way until there are 100(112–118) sts. Break off A and join in B. Now working in stripes of 6 rows B, 6 rows C, 6 rows B and 18 rows A cont as follows: Cont to inc as before until there are 128(140–146) sts. Work 1 row. [4th row of last C stripe completed] **Next row:** K 2 tog, k 61(67–70) sts, [M1R] twice, k to last 2 sts, k 2 tog. **Next row:** P. Rep last 2 rows 24 times more. [6th row of A stripe should now be completed] ** **Shape armholes and neck. Next row:** Cast off 5(7–7) sts, k 57(61–64) sts, k 2 tog, turn leaving rem sts on holder. Cont on these sts. Dec 1 st at each end of next 7 rows. Work 23 rows without shaping, ending with a k row. **Shape shoulder.** Keeping armhole edge straight, cast off at beg of next and foll alt rows 3 sts 4(3–2) times and 4 sts 3(4–5) times. Work 1 row. Cast off rem 20(23–25) sts.

Striped sweater

Rejoin wool to rem sts at neck edge. **Next row:** K 2 tog, k to last 5(7–7) sts, cast off 5(7–7) sts. Rejoin wool to rem sts at armhole edge. Dec 1 st at each end of next 7 rows. Work 22 rows without shaping, ending with a p row. Shape shoulder to match first side.

BACK: Work as given for Front from ** to **. **Shape armholes. Next row:** Cast off 5(7–7) sts, k 58(62–65) sts, including st already on needle, [M1R] twice, k to last 5(7–7) sts, cast off 5(7–7) sts. Turn and rejoin wool at armhole edge. Cont to inc in centre of work, dec 1 st at each end of next 7 rows. Work 2 rows inc in centre on first row. **Shape neck. Next row:** K 55(59–62) sts, k 2 tog, turn, leave rem sts on holder. Cont on these sts. Keeping armhole edge straight dec 1 st at neck edge on next 12 rows. Work 8 rows without shaping, ending with a k row. Shape shoulder as given for front. Rejoin wool to rem sts at neck edge, k 2 tog, k to end. Keeping armhole edge straight, dec 1 st at neck edge on next 12 rows. Work 7 rows without shaping, ending with a p row. Shape shoulder to match first side.

FRONT WELT: With No 11 needles and right side of work facing and with B, k up 86(94–98) sts along lower edge. Work 58 rows in k 1, p 1 rib. Cast off loosely in rib.

BACK WELT: Work as for Front Welt.

NECK BORDER: Press each piece lightly with warm iron and damp cloth. Join shoulder seams. With set of four No 11 double pointed needles and B k up 46 sts evenly along Back neck edge and 64 sts along Front neck edge. Work 10 rounds in k 1, p 1 rib. Cast off loosely in rib.

ARMHOLE BORDERS: With No 11 needles and B, k up 96 (100–100) sts round armhole edge. Work 5 rows k 1, p 1 rib. Cast off in rib.

TO MAKE UP: Join side seams using back st, including armhole borders. Press seams.

Cable bikini designed by Frances Easterling

Instructions are for a 34″ bust.

MATERIALS: 4 ozs of Twilleys Crysette. One pair Nos 13 and 14 needles. One cable needle. Shirring elastic. Two buttons.

Measurements: To fit a 34″ bust, 36″ hips.

TENSION: 7 sts and 9 rows to 1″ in reverse st-st No 13's.

TOP

FRONT CENTRE SECTION: With No 14 needles cast on 85 sts. Work in k 1, p 1 rib for 6 rows. Change to No 13 needles. **1st row:** [Right side] P 33, k 8, p 3, k 8, p 33. **2nd row:** K 33, p 8, k 3, p 8, k 33. Rep these 2 rows once more. **5th row:** P 33, sl next 4 sts on to cable needle and hold at back of work, k 4, then k 4 from cable needle [called C4B] p 3, C4B, p 33. **6th row:** Inc 1 st in first st, k 12, inc 1 st in next st, k 19, p 8, k 3, p 8, k 19, inc 1 st in next st, k 12, inc 1 st in last st. **7th row:** P 35, k 8, p 3, k 8, p 35. **8th row:** K 14, inc 1 st in next st, k 20, p 8, k 3, p 8, k 20, inc 1 st in next st, k 14. **9th row:** P 36, k 8, p 3, k 8, p 36. **10th row:** Inc 1 st in first st, k 13, inc 1 st in next st, k 21, p 8, k 3, p 8, k 21, inc 1 st in next st, k 13, inc 1 st in last st. **11th row:** P 38, C4B, p 3, C4B, p 38. **12th row:** K 15, inc 1 st in next st, k 22, p 8, k 3, p 8, k 22, inc 1 st in next st, k 15. **13th row:** P 39, k 8, p 3, k 8, p 39. **14th row:** Inc 1 st in first st, k 14, inc 1 st in next st, k 23, p 8, k 3, p 8, k 23, inc 1 st in next st, k 14, inc 1 st in last st.

15th row: P 41, k 8, p 3, k 8, p 41. **16th row:** K 41, p 8, k 3, p 8, k 41. [101 sts] Rep last 2 rows twice more. **21st row:** P 41, C4B, p 3, C4B, p 41. **22nd row:** K 16, sl 1, k 1, psso, k 23, p 8, k 3, p 8, k 23, k 2 tog, k 16. **23rd row:** P 40, k 8, p 3, k 8, p 40. **24th row:** K 2 tog, k 14, sl 1, k 1, psso, k 22, p 8, k 3, p 8, k 22, k 2 tog, k 14, k 2 tog. **25th row:** P 38, k 8, p 3, k 8, p 38. **26th row:** K 15, sl 1, k 1, psso, k 21, p 8, k 3, p 8, k 21, k 2 tog, k 15. **27th row:** P 37, k 8, p 3, k 8, p 37. **28th row:** K 2 tog, k 13, sl 1, k 1, psso, k 20, p 8, k 3, p 8, k 20, k 2 tog, k 13, k 2 tog, **29th row:** P 35, k 8, p 3, k 8, p 35. [89 sts] **30th row:** K 35, p 8, k 3, p 8, k 35. **31st row:** P 35, C4B, p 3, C4B, p 35. **32nd row:** As 30th. **33rd row:** As 29th. **34th row:** As 30th. **35th row:** P 35, k 8, p 3, k 8, p 21, turn. **36th row:** K 21, p 8, k 3, p 8, k 21, turn. **37th row:** P 21, k 8, p 3, k 8, p 16, turn. **38th row:** K 16, p 8, k 3, p 8, k 16, turn. **39th row:** P 16, k 8, p 1, place rem 45 sts on holder. Cast on 6 sts, p these 6 sts, k 1, p 8, k 1, place rem 34 sts on holder. Cont on these 16 sts only for first shoulder strap. **41st row:** P 1, C4B, p 1, k 6. **42nd row:** P 6, k 1, p 8, k 1. **43rd row:** P 1, k 8, p 1, k 6. Rep these 2 rows working cable row on every 10th row. Cont until work measures 18″ from divided cable. Cast off. **2nd cable.** With right side of cable facing take 11 sts at centre from holder. Leave rem 34 sts on holder. Cast on 5 sts for facing at centre [between cables], k 6, p 1, C4B, p 1. Cont working as for first

Cable bikini

cable for 18″. Cast off.

LEFT SIDE: With No 14 needles cast on 63 sts and work in k 1, p 1 rib for 6 rows. Change to No 13 needles. **1st row:** K 59, p 4. **2nd row:** K 4, p 59. Rep these 2 rows 6 times more. **15th row:** Inc 1 st at beg of row. Work 3 more rows. Inc 1 st at beg of next row. Cont without shaping until work measures 2¼″ from cast-on edge, ending with a p row. **Next row:** K to last 25 sts turn patt to end. **Next row:** K to last 35 sts, turn, patt to end. **Next row:** K to last 45 sts, turn, patt to end. Cont in this way until 10 sts rem. Leave all sts on holder.

RIGHT SIDE: Work as for Left side, reversing shaping.

LEFT RIBBED EDGE: With No 14 needles and right side facing, take the left side at the top, k 4 sts, p 61 sts, then take Front section and p across sts on holder on left side. Work in k 1, p 1 rib for 6 rows. Cast off. Work right ribbed edge in same way reversing shaping.

TO MAKE UP: Press with a damp cloth and warm iron. Join side seams. Turn back facing of cable straps and st to outside edge. Make loops at end of each strap. Turn back facings on right and left sides [back over-wrap] and sew on hooks and eyes.

PANTS

Beg at top of Back. With No 13 needles cast on 98 sts. Work in reverse st-st for 46 rows. Cast off 5 sts at beg of next 6 rows. Cast off 2 sts at beg of next 4 rows. Dec 1 st at each end of next and every foll alt row 20 times in all. Work 10 rows without shaping. Inc 1 st at each end of next and foll 4th row. Work 4 rows without shaping. Inc 1 st at each end of next and every foll alt row 10 times in all. Inc 1 st at each end of next 30 rows. Work 58 rows without shaping. Cast off.

CABLE INSERTIONS: [Make two] With No 13 needles cast on 21 sts. **1st row:** P 1, k 8, p 3, k 8, p 1. **2nd row:** K 1, p 8, k 3, p 8, k 1. Rep these 2 rows once more and 1st row once. **6th row:** P 1, C4B, p 3, C4B, p 1. Cont in this way working cable on every 10th row until work measures 3½″. **Divide cables.** P 1, k 8, p 2 tog, turn and work this side only until single cable measures 10½″ to make edging for legs of Bikini. K other 10 sts of cable to correspond.

TO MAKE UP: Sew inserts of double cable to back and front of st-st sides [easing slightly to fit]. Sew divided cable around legs grafting tog cables where they meet. **Top edging.** With No 14 needles k up 208 sts and work 12 rows k 1, p 1 rib. Cast off. Thread shirring elastic through top if required.

Lace stitch bikini

Instructions are for a 34″ bust, 36″ hips. Changes for 36″ bust, 38″ hips are given in brackets.

MATERIALS: 3(3) balls of Wendy Invitation Crochet Cotton in White, A; 3(3) balls of same in contrast, B. One pair No 12 needles. 2½ yards round elastic.

MEASUREMENTS: To fit a 34″(36″) bust; 36″(38″) hips.

TENSION: 8 sts and 10 rows to 1″.

TOP

With No 12 needles and A, cast on 50(54) sts. **1st row:** K. **2nd row:** P 2 tog, p to last 2 sts, p 2 tog tbl. Rep these 2 rows 3(4) times more. **Commence patt. 1st row:** K 6(7), [y fwd, sl 1, k 1, psso] 4 times, * k 3, [y fwd, sl 1, k 1, psso] 4 times; rep from * once more, k 6(7). **2nd and every even row:** P 2 tog, p to last 2 sts, p 2 tog tbl. **3rd row:** K 6(7), [y fwd, sl 1, k 1, psso] 3 times, * k 5, [y fwd, sl 1, k 1, psso] 3 times; rep from * once more, k 6(7). **5th row:** K 6(7), [y fwd, sl 1, k 1, psso] twice, * k 7, [y fwd, sl 1, k 1, psso] twice; rep from * once more, k 6(7). **7th row:** K 6(7), y fwd, sl 1, k 1, psso, * k 9, y fwd, sl 1, k 1, psso; rep from * once more, k 6(7).

9th row: K 8(9), [y fwd, sl 1, k 1, psso] 4 times, k 3, [y fwd, sl 1, k 1, psso] 4 times, k 7(8). **11th row:** K 8(9), [y fwd, sl 1, k 1, psso] 3 times, k 5, [y fwd, sl 1, k 1, psso] 3 times, k 7(8). **13th row:** K 8(9), [y fwd, sl 1, k 1, psso] twice, k 7, [y fwd, sl 1, k 1, psso] twice, k 7(8). **15th row:** K 8(9), y fwd, sl 1, k 1, psso, k 9, y fwd, sl 1, k 1, psso, k 7(8). **17th row:** K 10(11), [y fwd, sl 1, k 1, psso] 4 times, k 8(9). **19th row:** K 10(11), [y fwd, sl 1, k 1, psso] 3 times, k 8(9). **21st row:** K 10(11), [y fwd, sl 1, k 1, psso] twice, k 8(9). **23rd row:** K 10(11), y fwd, sl 1, k 1, psso, k 8(9). **24th row:** As 2nd. Now work 16(18) more rows in st-st, dec as before on every p row. K tog 2 rem sts. Fasten off. Work another piece in exactly the same way.

STRAPS: [Make two] With No 12 needles and B, cast on 6 sts. **1st row:** K 1, inc 1 st by picking up loop from between needles and p into back of it, k 1, p 1, inc 1 st by picking up loop and k into back of it, p 1, k 1, inc 1 st by picking up loop and p into back of it, k 1. [9 sts] Cont in rib. **1st row:** K 2, * p 1, k 1; rep from * to last st, k 1. **2nd row:** * K 1, p 1; rep from * to last st, k 1. Rep these 2 rows until strap measures 40″(42″) when slightly stretched. Cast off firmly in rib.

BORDERS: [Make two] With No 12 needles and B, cast on 6 sts and work inc row as given for straps. Work 6″(6½″) in rib. Cast off firmly in rib.

TO MAKE UP: Press each piece lightly with warm iron and damp cloth. Sew borders to cast-on edges of cup pieces. Leaving an equal amount at each end for ties, pin straps in position as illustration; the first strap to lower edge of right cup and top edge of left cup; the 2nd strap to top edge of right cup and lower edge of left cup and with 2nd strap overlapping first strap at centre. Sew on by backstitching. Press seams lightly.

PANTS

BACK: ** With No 12 needles and A, cast on 137(146) sts. **1st row:** K. **2nd row:** P. Cont in patt. **1st row:** K 4(3), [y fwd, sl 1, k 1, psso] 4 times, * k 3, [y fwd, sl 1, k 1, psso] 4 times; rep from * to last 4(3) sts, k 4(3). **2nd and every alt row:** P. **3rd row:** K 5(4), [y fwd, sl 1, k 1, psso] 3 times, k 1, * k 4, [y fwd, sl 1, k 1, psso] 3 times, k 1; rep from * to last 4(3) sts, k 4(3). **5th row:** K 6(5), [y fwd, sl 1, k 1, psso] twice, k 2, * k 5, [y fwd, sl 1, k 1, psso] twice, k 2; rep from * to last 4(3) sts, k 4(3). **7th row:** K 7(6), y fwd, sl 1, k 1, psso, k 3, * k 6, y fwd, sl 1, k 1, psso, k 3; rep from * to last 4(3) sts, k 4(3). **9th row:** K 10(9), * [y fwd, sl 1, k 1, psso] 4 times, k 3; rep from * to last 6(5) sts, k 6(5). **11th row:** K 10(9), * k 1, [y fwd, sl 1, k 1, psso] 3 times, k 4; rep from * to last 6(5) sts, k 6(5). **13th row:** K 10(9), * k 2, [y fwd, sl 1, k 1, psso] twice, k 5; rep from * to last 6(5) sts, k 6(5). **15th row:** K 10(9), * k 3, y fwd, sl 1, k 1, psso, k 6; rep from * to last 6(5) sts, k 6(5). **16th row:** P. Cont in st-st. Work 4 rows. **. **Shape legs.** Cast off 3 sts at beg of next 18(20) rows and 2 sts at beg of foll 16 rows. Dec 1 st at beg of every row until 23(24) sts rem. Work 2 rows. Cast off.

FRONT: Work as for Back from ** to **. **Shape legs.** Cast off 36 sts at beg of first 2 rows, 3 sts at beg of next 6(8) rows and 2 sts at beg of foll 6(6) rows. Dec 1 st at beg of every row until 23(24) sts rem. Work 2 rows. Cast off.

WAIST BORDER: With No 12 needles and B cast on 6 sts and work inc row as given for straps of top. Cont in rib until border measures 32″(34″) when slightly stretched. Cast off firmly in rib.

LEG BORDERS: [Make two] Work 18″(19″) as for waist border.

TO MAKE UP: Press each piece lightly with warm iron and damp cloth. Sew side and crutch seams. Join narrow edge of borders. Pin borders in position, sew on by backstitching. Press seams lightly. Thread elastic through knitting at waist and legs and fasten ends securely.

Shawl and handbag

MATERIALS: 14 50-grm balls of Patons Doublet. One pair No 2 needles. One crochet hook, International size 5·00.

TENSION: 3 sts and 4½ rows to 1″ over patt on No 2 needles.

With No 2 needles cast on 259 sts. **1st row:** K 1, sl 1, k 1, psso, k to last 3 sts, k 2 tog, k 1. **2nd row:** K 1, p 2 tog, p to last 3 sts, p 2 tog tbl, k 1. Cont in st-st dec 1 st at each end of every row in this way until 5 sts rem. **Next row:** K 1, sl 2 p-wise, k 1, p 2sso, k 1. **Next row:** K 3 tog. Fasten off.

BORDER: Join wool to right shaped edge at cast on edge, and, with crochet hook, work a row of dc along the 2 shaped edges, and then along the cast on edge, working 1 dc for each row along the shaped edges, 1 dc into st at point, and 2 dc for each 3 sts along cast on edge. Join with a sl st. Do not turn. **Next row:** * 7 ch, miss 3 sts, 1 dc into next st; rep from * along shaped edges only, and missing 2 sts instead of 3 at each side of point. Turn with 7 ch. **Next row:** * 1 dc into centre ch of 7 ch loop, 7 ch; rep from * ending with 1 dc into sl st. Turn with 7 ch. Rep last row twice more, but working twice into loop at point and working last dc into centre ch of turning ch loop. Fasten off.

TO MAKE UP: Pin out shawl in the form of a triangle, stretching the shaped edges as necessary. Press. **Fringe.** Using four strands of wool 15″ long for each tassel work a fringe along the shaped edges, working a tassel into each 7 ch loop. Trim ends.

Handbag

MATERIALS: 4 ozs Robin Crepe Double Knitting in main shade, A; 4 ozs in contrast, B; 3 ozs in contrast, C. One pair each Nos 5 and 8 needles. One No 9 crochet hook, International size 3·50. Three 1″ diameter rings.

MEASUREMENTS: Bag measures approx 11½″ × 11½″.

TENSION: 4½ sts to 1″.

NOTE: (A) Sl all sts p-wise carrying yarn loosely at back of sts on right-side rows. Sl all sts p-wise carrying yarn loosely in front of sts on wrong side rows. **(B)** Do not break off wool when changing colour but carry it up side of work when not in use.

USE DOUBLE WOOL THROUGHOUT.

With No 8 needles and A, cast on 43 sts. **1st row:** * K 1, p 1; rep from * to last st, k 1. Rep this row 7 times more. Break off A. Change to No 5 needles. **Commence patt. 1st row:** With B, k. **2nd row:** As 1st. **3rd row:** With C, k 3, * [sl 1, k 1] twice, sl 1, k 3; rep from * to end. **4th row:** With C, p 3, * [sl 1, k 1] twice, sl 1, p 3; rep from * to end. **5th row:** With B, k 1, sl 2, * k 5, sl 3; rep from * ending k 5, sl 2, k 1. **6th row:** With B, k 1, sl 2, * k 5, sl 3; rep from * ending k 5, sl 2, k 1. **7th row:** With C, as 3rd. **8th row:** With C, as 4th. **9th row:** With B, as 1st. **10th row:** With B, as 2nd. **11th row:** With C, [k 1, sl 1] twice, * k 3, [sl 1, k 1] twice, sl 1; rep from * ending k 3, [sl 1, k 1] twice. **12th row:** With C, [k 1, sl 1] twice, * p 3, [sl 1, k 1] twice, sl 1; rep from * ending p 3, [sl 1, k 1] twice. **13th row:** With B, k 4, * sl 3, k 5; rep from * ending k 4 instead of k 5. **14th row:** With B, k 4, * sl 3, k 5; rep from * ending k 4 instead of k 5. **15th row:** With C, as 11th. **16th row:** With C, as 12th. These 16 rows form patt. Rep patt rows 6 times more, then 1st and 2nd rows once. Break off B and C, join in A. Cont with No 8 needles. **Next row:** K. **Next row:** * K 1, p 1; rep from * to last st, k 1. Rep last row 7 times more. Cast off in patt.

WORK BORDER: With No 8 needles and right side of work facing and A, pick up and k 67 sts along one side edge, working 1 st for each 2 rows and 1 st for cast off row. **Next row:** * K 1, p 1; rep from * to last st, k 1. Rep this row 7 times more. Cast off in patt. Work border along other side edge in same way. Make another piece the same, but rep 16 patt rows 4 times instead of 6 and pick up 51 sts along side edges.

TO MAKE UP: Press each piece lightly with warm iron and damp cloth. Place two pieces tog with wrong sides of work towards each other, and cast-on edges matching. With A, saddle st through both thicknesses along side and cast-on edges. Make buttonloop in centre of cast off edge of flap as follows: Join wool A with a dc into edge, work 8 ch, leave space, work 1 dc into edge; fasten off.

BUTTON: Using crochet hook and double wool in A, work a row of dc firmly all round one ring. Break wool, leaving two ends. Thread these ends on to a needle, thread through each st right round ring. Draw up tightly to centre of ring and fasten with several sts. Sew button to bag to match loop.

STRAP RINGS: With double wool, work a row of dc firmly round 2 rem rings, leaving ends for sewing. Sew a ring to each side of bag at opening edge.

STRAP: With No 8 needles and A, cast on 5 sts. **1st row:** [K 1, p 1] twice, k 1. Rep this row until strap measures 36″, when slightly stretched lengthwise. Cast off in patt. Sew ends of straps to rings.

Gloves and socks

Gloves

MATERIALS: 1 oz each of contrasting colours A, B, C, D and E in Robin Vogue 4-ply. One pair No 11 needles.
RIGHT HAND: ** With No 11 needles and A, cast on 54 sts. **1st row:** * P 2, k 2; rep from * to last 2 sts, p 2. **2nd row:** * K 2, p 2; rep from * to last 2 sts, k 2. These two rows form patt. Work 4 more rows. Break off A and join in E. **Next row:** K. **Next row:** As 2nd patt row. Break off E and join in A. **Next row:** K. **Next row:** As 2nd patt row. Work 10 more rows in patt. Break off A and join in E. **Next row:** K. **Next row:** As 2nd patt row. Break off E. Join in A. **Next row:** K. **Next row:** As 2nd patt row. Work 4 more rows in patt. Break off A and join in B and cont in st-st. Work 10 rows. ** **Shape thumb. 1st row:** K 29 sts, inc 1 st by picking up loop between needles and k into back of it, k 2, inc 1, k to end. **2nd row:** P. Break off B and join in C. **3rd row:** K. **4th row:** P 23 sts, inc 1 st by picking up loop from between needles and p into back of it, p 4, inc 1, p to end. Break off C and join in B. **5th row:** K. **6th row:** P. **7th row:** K 29 sts, inc 1 st as before, k 6, inc 1, k to end. **8th row:** P. **9th row:** K. **10th row:** P 23, inc 1 st as before, p 8, inc 1, p to end. Break off B and join in D. Cont to inc in this way on every 3rd row, working 6 rows D, 6 rows B and 2 rows C. [70 sts] Break off C and join in B. **Commence thumb. 1st row:** K 47 sts, turn and cast on 2 sts. **2nd row:** P 20, turn and cast on 2 sts. Cont on these 22 sts. Work 4 more rows in B, 2 rows C, 6 rows B, 6 rows E and 2 rows D. **Shape top. 1st row:** * K 2 tog; rep from * to end. **2nd row:** P. **3rd row:** * K 2 tog; rep from * to last st, k 1. Break off wool leaving enough to thread through sts, draw up and fasten off. Sew seam to base of thumb. With right side of work facing and B, using right-hand needle pick up and k 3 sts at base of thumb, k to end. Cont on these 55 sts. Work 5 more rows B, 6 rows E and 6 rows D. Break off D and join in B. **First finger. Next row:** K 35, turn and cast on 2 sts. **Next row:** P 17, turn and cast on 2 sts. Cont on these 19 sts. Work 4 more rows B, 2 rows C, 6 rows B, 6 rows E and 6 rows D. Break off D and join in B. **Shape top. 1st row:** * K 2 tog; rep from * to last st, k 1. **2nd row:** P. **3rd row:** * K 2 tog; rep from * to end. Break off wool and complete as for thumb. **2nd finger.** With right side of work

facing and B, using right hand needle pick up and k 3 sts at base of 1st finger, k 7, turn, cast on 2 sts. **Next row:** P 19, turn, cast on 2 sts. Cont on these 21 sts. Work 4 more rows B, 2 rows C, 6 rows B, 6 rows E, 6 rows D and 2 rows B. **Shape top. 1st row:** * K 2 tog; rep from * to last st, k 1. **2nd row:** P. **3rd row:** As 1st. Break wool and complete to match thumb. **3rd finger.** With right side of work facing and B, using right-hand needle, pick up and k 3 sts at base of 2nd finger, k 6, turn, cast on 2 sts. **Next row:** P 17 sts, turn, cast on 2 sts. Complete to match first finger. **4th finger.** With right side of work facing and B, using right-hand needle, pick up and k 3 sts at base of 3rd finger, k to end. **Next row:** P 17. Cont on these 17 sts. Work 4 more rows in B, 2 rows C, 6 rows B, 6 rows E and 2 rows D. **Shape top. 1st row:** * K 2 tog; rep from * to last st, k 1. **2nd row:** P. **3rd row:** As 1st. Break wool and complete as for thumb, sewing along side of glove to the cast-on edge. Press lightly with warm iron and damp cloth.
LEFT HAND: Follow instructions for Right Hand from ** to **. **Shape thumb. 1st row:** K 23, inc 1 st, k 2, inc 1, k to end. **2nd row:** P. Break off B and join in C. **3rd row:** K. **4th row:** P 29, inc 1 st, p 4, inc 1 st, p to end. Cont to inc on every 3rd row, working in stripes as for Right-hand to beg of thumb. **Next row:** K 41 sts, turn, cast on 2 sts. **Next row:** P 20 sts, turn, cast on 2 sts. Complete thumb and fingers as for Right hand. Press lightly with warm iron and damp cloth.

Long socks

MATERIALS: 1 oz of Robin Vogue 4-ply in main shade, A; 3 ozs in contrast, B; 1 oz each of contrasts C and D; 2 ozs in contrast, E. One pair each Nos 10 and 11 needles. $\frac{3}{4}$ yd round elastic.
With No 10 needles and A, cast on 78 sts. **1st row:** P 2, k 2; rep from * to last 2 sts, p 2. **2nd row:** * K 2, p 2; rep from * to last 2 sts, k 2. These two rows form patt. Work 10 more rows. Break off A and join in B. **Next row:** K. **Next row:** As 2nd patt row. Work 10 more rows in patt. Break off B and join in C. Now k the first row on each change of colour, cont in stripes as folls; 2 rows C, 12 rows B, 2 rows C, 6 rows B, 6 rows D, 6 rows B, 12 rows A, 6 rows B, 2 rows C, 6 rows B, 6 rows

D, 6 rows B, 2 rows C, 6 rows B, 6 rows E, 16 rows A and 6 rows E. Change to No 11 needles and cont in stripes of 12 rows B, 2 rows C, 6 rows B, 16 rows E, 6 rows B and 5 rows D. **Next row:** With D, k 2 tog, patt to last 2 sts, k 2 tog. Break off D. With right side of work facing, sl first 19 sts on to a holder, join in B and k over centre 38 sts, sl rem 19 sts on to a holder. **Work instep.** Work 5 more rows in B. Cont in stripes of 2 rows C, 6 rows B, 6 rows D, 6 rows B, 6 rows D, 6 rows B, 2 rows C and 8 rows B. [Adjust length of foot here] Break off B and join in E. **Next row:** K 3, * k 2 tog, k 4; rep from * to last 5 sts, k 2 tog, k 3. [32 sts] **Next row:** P. **Shape toe. 1st row:** K 1, sl 1, k 1, psso, k to last 3 sts, k 2 tog, k 1. **2nd row:** P. Rep last 2 rows 8 times more. Break off wool and leave rem 14 sts on a holder. Return to heel sts and slip 2 sets of sts on to one No 11 needle with outside edges to centre. [38 sts] Join in E. **Shape heel. 1st row:** [Right side] Sl 1, k 36 sts, turn. **2nd row:** Sl 1, p 35 sts, turn. **3rd row:** Sl 1, k 34 sts, turn. **4th row:** Sl 1, p 33 sts, turn. Cont working 1 st less on each row until 11 sts rem unworked on each side. [Last row will be sl 1, p 15] Turn and cont as folls: **1st row:** Sl 1, k 15, pick up strand of wool from between needles on to left-hand needle and k this loop tog with next st, [thus preventing a hole], turn. **2nd row:** Sl 1, p 16, pick up strand between needles and p tog with next st, turn. Cont in this way working one more st on each row until 38 sts are on one row. Break off E and join in D. **Next row:** K 3, * k 2 tog, k 4; rep from * to last 5 sts, k 2 tog, k 3. [32 sts] **Next row:** P. Cont in st-st until work measures same as instep to beg of toe shaping, ending with a p row. Break off D and join in E. Work 2 rows. Shape toe as for instep. Graft or cast off 2 sets of sts tog.

TO MAKE UP: Pin out and press each sock. Join foot and leg seams. Cut two lengths of elastic and thread through knitting at cast on edges. Join ends firmly. Press seams lightly.

Short socks

MATERIALS: 1 oz of Robin Vogue 4-ply in main shade. A; 2 ozs of same in contrast, B; 1 oz each of same in contrasts C and D. One pair No 11 needles. ½ yd round elastic.

With No 11 needles and A cast on 78 sts. **1st row:** * P 2, k 2; rep from * to last 2 sts, p 2. **2nd row:** * K 2, p 2; rep from * to last 2 sts, k 2. These two rows form patt. Work 10 more rows. Break off A and join in B. **Next row:** K. **Next row:** As 2nd patt row. Cont in patt. Work until sock measures 5½″ from cast on edge, ending with 1st patt row. **Next row:** K 2 tog, patt to last 2 sts, k 2 tog. Break off wool. With right side of work facing, sl first 19 sts on to a holder, rejoin wool and work in patt over centre 38 sts, sl rem 19 sts on to a holder. Cont in patt for instep on centre 38 sts for 5″, ending with 2nd patt row. [Adjust length here if required] Break off B and join in C. **Next row:** K 3, * k 2 tog, k 4; rep from * to last 5 sts, k 2 tog, k 3. [32 sts] **Next row:** P. **Shape toe. 1st row:** K 1, sl 1, k 1, psso, k to last 3 sts, k 2 tog, k 1. **2nd row:** P. Rep last 2 rows 8 times more. Break off wool and leave rem 14 sts on a holder. Return to heel sts, sl 2 sets of sts on to 1 needle with outside edges to the centre. [38 sts] Join in D. **Shape heel. 1st row:** [Right side] Sl 1, k 36 sts, turn. **2nd row:** Sl 1, p 35 sts, turn. **3rd row:** Sl 1, k 34 sts, turn. **4th row:** Sl 1, p 33 sts, turn. Cont working 1 st less on each row in this way until 11 sts rem unworked at each side. [Last row will be sl 1, p 15] Turn and cont as folls: **1st row:** Sl 1, k 15, pick up strand of wool between needles on to left-hand needle and k this loop tog with next st [thus preventing a hole], turn. **2nd row:** Sl 1, p 16, pick up strand between needles and p tog with next st, turn. Cont in this way working 1 st more on each row until 38 sts are again on 1 row. Break off D and join in B. **Next row:** K 3, * k 2 tog, k 4; rep from * to last 5 sts, k 2 tog, k 3. [32 sts] **Next row:** P. Cont in st-st until work measures same as instep to beg of toe, ending with a p row. Break off B and join in C. Work 2 rows. Shape toe as for instep. Graft or cast off 2 sets of sts tog.

TO MAKE UP: Pin out and press each sock. Join foot and leg seams. Cut two lengths of elastic and thread through knitting at cast-on edges. Join ends firmly. Press seams lightly.

Child's cable sweater

Instructions are for a 24″ chest. Changes for 26″ and 28″ sizes are given in brackets.

MATERIALS: 6(7–8) ozs of Jaeger Celtic Spun. One pair each Nos 7 and 10 needles.

MEASUREMENTS: To fit a 24″(26″–28″) chest. Length at centre back: 14½″(15½″–16½″), adjustable. Sleeve seam: 11″(12″–13″), adjustable.

TENSION: 7 sts and 7½ rows to 1″ over patt on No 7 needles.

FRONT: ** With No 10 needles cast on 73(79–85) sts. **1st row:** K 2, * p 1, k 1; rep from * to last st, k 1. **2nd row:** * K 1, p 1; rep from * to last st, k 1. Rep 1st and 2nd rows once more, then 1st row once. **Next row:** K into front and back of first st, * p 5, k into front and back of next st; rep from * to end. [86(93–100) sts] Change to No 7 needles. **Commence patt. 1st row:** P 2, * sl 1 p-wise with wool at back of st, k 4, p 2; rep from * to end. **2nd row:** K 2, * p 4, sl 1 p-wise with wool at front of st, k 2; rep from * to end. **3rd row:** P 2, * drop sl-st to front of work, k 2, pick up dropped st and k it, k 2, p 2; rep from * to end. **4th row:** K 2, * p 5, k 2; rep from * to end. **5th row:** P 2, * k 4, sl 1 p-wise with wool at back of st, p 2; rep from * to end. **6th row:** K 2, * sl 1 p-wise with wool at front of st, p 4, k 2; rep from * to end. **7th row:** P 2, * k 2, sl 2 p-wise with wool at back of sts, drop sl-st to front of work, sl same 2 sts back to left-hand needle, pick up dropped st and k it, k 2, p 2; rep from * to end. **8th row:** As 4th. These eight rows form patt. Work until front measures 9½″(10″–10½″) from beg, or required length to underarm, ending with a wrong side row. **Shape armholes.** Cast off 5(6–7) sts at beg of next 2 rows. Dec 1 st at beg of every row until 68(71–74) sts rem. ** Cont without shaping until armholes measure 3½″(4″–4½″) from beg, ending with a right side row. **Shape neck. Next row:** Patt 26(27–28) sts, cast off 16(17–18) sts, patt to end. Cont on last set of sts as folls: Keeping armhole edge straight, dec 1 st at neck edge on next 6 rows, then on foll 3 alt rows, ending at armhole edge. **Shape shoulder.** Keeping neck edge straight, cast off 5(6–7) sts at beg of next row, and 6 sts at beg of foll alt row. Work 1 row. Cast off rem 6(6–6) sts. Rejoin wool to rem sts at neck edge. Keeping armhole edge straight dec 1 st at neck edge on next 6 rows. Then on foll 3 alt rows. Work 1 row ending at armhole edge. Shape shoulder to match first side.

BACK: Work as given for Front from ** to **. Work until armholes measure same as Front to beg of shoulder shaping, ending with a wrong side row. **Shape shoulders and back neck. Next row:** Cast off 5(6–7) sts, patt 15(15–15) sts, cast off 28(29–30) sts, patt to end. Cont on last set of sts. **1st row:** Cast off 5(6–7) sts, patt to last 2 sts, dec 1 st. **2nd row:** Dec 1 st, patt to end. **3rd row:** Cast off 6(6–6) sts, patt to last 2 sts, dec 1 st. **4th row:** Work in patt. Cast off rem 6(6–6) sts. Rejoin wool to rem sts at neck edge. **1st row:** Dec 1 st, patt to end. **2nd row:** Cast off 6(6–6) sts, patt to last 2 sts, dec 1 st. **3rd row:** As 1st. Cast off rem 6(6–6) sts.

SLEEVES: With No 10 needles cast on 43(45–49) sts. Work 5 rows in ribbing as given for Front. **Next row:** [Sizes 24″ and 28″ only] K into front and back of first st, * p 5, k into front and back of next st; rep from * to end. **Next row:** [26″ size only] P into front and back of first st, p 3, * k into front and back of next st, p 5; rep from * ending last rep, p into front and back of last st. [51(54–58) sts] Change to No 7 needles. **Commence patt. 1st row:** [Sizes 24″ and 28″ only] P 2, * sl 1 p-wise with wool at back of st, k 4, p 2; rep from * to end. **1st row:** [26″ size only] * Sl 1 p-wise with wool at back of st, k 4, p 2; rep from * to last 5 sts, sl 1 p-wise, k 4. This sets patt. Work 7 more rows. Keeping patt correct, inc 1 st at each end of next and every foll 6th row until there are 71(76–82) sts. Cont without shaping until sleeve measures 11″(12″–13″) from beg, or required length to underarm, ending with a wrong side row. **Shape top.** Cast off 5(6–7) sts at beg of next 2 rows and 2(2–2) sts at beg of foll 4 rows. Dec 1 st at beg of every row until 43(44–44) sts rem. Cast off at beg of next and foll rows, 2 sts 4 times, 3 sts twice and 4 sts twice. Cast off rem 21(22–22) sts.

NECK BORDER: Press each piece lightly with a warm iron and damp cloth. Join left shoulder seam. With No 10 needles k up 37(38–39) sts along back neck edge, 17(17–17) sts down left side of neck to cast off sts, 16(17–18) sts from cast off sts at centre front and 17 (17–17) sts up right side of neck. **1st row:** * K 1, p 1; rep from * to last st, k 1. **2nd row:** K 2, * p 1, k 1; rep from * to last st, k 1. Rep 1st and 2nd rows 3 times more, then 1st row once. Cast off loosely in rib.

TO MAKE UP: Join right shoulder seam and neck border seam. Sew sleeves into armholes. Join side and sleeve seams. Press seams lightly.

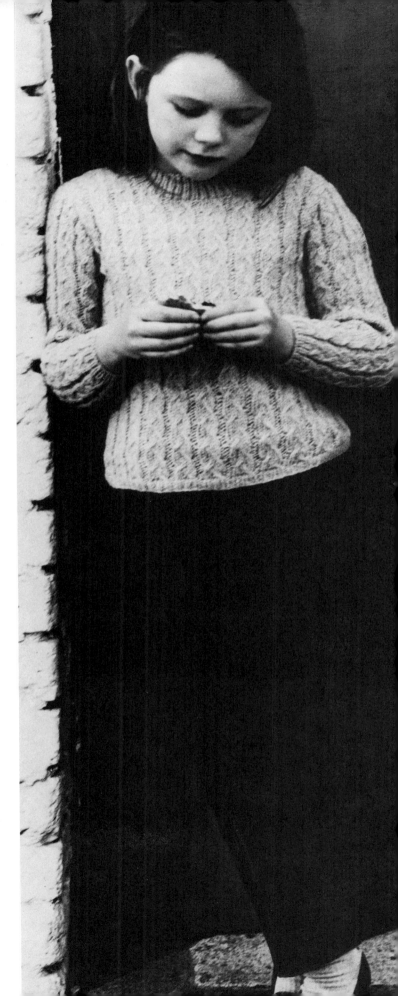

Child's Fair Isle

Instructions are for a 26″ chest. Changes for 28″, 30″ and 32″ sizes are given in brackets.

MATERIALS: 8(9–9–10) ozs of Lee Target Motoravia 4-ply in main shade, A; 1 oz each of contrasts B, C, D, E and F. One pair each Nos 10 and 12 needles. One set of four Nos 10 and 12 needles, pointed at both ends.

MEASUREMENTS: To fit a 26″(28″–30″–32″) chest. Length to shoulder: 16½″(18″–19½″–21″), adjustable. Sleeve seam: 13″(14″–15″–16″), adjustable.

TENSION: 7 sts to 1″ over st-st on No 10 needles.

SWEATER

BACK: With No 12 needles and A, cast on 99(107–113–121) sts. Work 1″ k 1, p 1 rib. Change to No 10 needles. **Commence Fair Isle patt. 1st row:** [Wrong side] With A, p to end. Beg with a k row, work rows 1 to 23 as given on chart, noting that 1st size will beg and end at point marked C, 2nd size will beg and end at point marked A, 3rd size will beg and end at point marked D and 4th size will beg and end at point marked B. **Next row:** Break off contrast colours, with A only p to end, inc 1 st in centre of row on 1st and 3rd sizes only. 100(107–114–121) sts. Beg with a k row cont in st-st until work measures 11″(12″–13″–14″) from beg, or required length to underarm, ending with a p row. **Shape armholes.** Cast off 6 sts at beg of next 2 rows. ** **Next row:** K 1, sl 1, k 1, psso, k to last 3 sts, k 2 tog, k 1. **Next row:** P. Rep last 2 rows 2(3–4–5) times more. ** 82(87–92–97) sts. Leave sts on holder for yoke.

FRONT: Work as given for Back.

SLEEVES: With No 12 needles and A, cast on 47(49–51–53) sts. Work 1″ k 1, p 1 rib. Change to No 10 needles. **Commence Fair Isle patt. 1st row:** [Wrong side] With A, p to end. Beg with a k row work rows 1 to 23 as given on chart, noting that 1st size will beg and end at point marked A, 2nd size will beg and end at point marked B, 3rd size will beg and end at point marked C and 4th size will beg and end at point marked D, **at the same time,** inc 1 st at each end of 7th and every foll 6th row. **Next row:** Break off contrast colours. With A only, p to end. Beg with a k row, cont in st-st, inc 1 st at each end of every 6th row as before until there are 75(79–83–87) sts. Cont without shaping until sleeve measures 13″(14″–15″–16″) from beg, or required length to underarm, ending with a p row. **Shape top.** Cast off 6 sts at beg of next 2 rows. Work from ** to ** as given for Back. 57(59–61–63) sts. Leave sts on holder.

sweater and beret

YOKE: Join raglan seams using back st. With set of four No 10 needles and A, k across all sts on holders, k 2 tog at each raglan seam and, on **1st size only**, inc 1 st at centre back and front; on **3rd size only**, dec 1 st at centre back and front; on **4th size only** dec 1 st at centre back and front and at centre of each sleeve. [276 (288–300–312) sts] Arrange sts on three needles so that round commences at centre back. **Commence Fair Isle patt.** Beg with a k row, work rounds 1 to 20 as given on chart noting that yoke on all sizes will beg at point marked B. **21st round:** [Dec round] K 2 in patt, * k 2 tog, k 4; rep from * to last 4 sts, k 2 tog, k 2. [230(240–250–260) sts] **22nd round.** Work as given on chart. **23rd round:** Work as given on chart. **24th round:** [Dec round] K 5, * k 2 tog, k 8; rep from * to last 5 sts, k 2 tog, k 3. [207(216–225–234) sts] Work rounds 25–33 as given on chart. **34th round:** [Dec round] K 6, * k 2 tog, k 7; rep from * to last 3 sts, k 2 tog, k 1. [184(192–200–208) sts] **35th round:** Work as given on chart. **36th round:** Work as given on chart. **37th round:** [Dec round] K 1, * k 2 tog, k 2; rep from * to last 3 sts, k 2 tog, k 1. [138(144–150–156) sts] Work rounds 38 to 40 as given on chart. **41st round:** [Dec round] K 2, * k 2 tog, k 4; rep from * to last 4 sts, k 2 tog, k 2. [115(120–125–130) sts] Work rounds 42 to 44 as given on chart. **45th round:** [Dec round] K 1, * k 2 tog, k 3; rep from * to last 4 sts, k 2 tog, k 2. [92(96–100–104) sts] **46th round:** Work as given on chart. **47th round:** Work as given on chart. Break off contrast colours. With A only k 1(1–3–5) rounds. Change to set of four No 12 needles. Work 2″ k 1, p 1 rib. Cast off loosely in rib.

TO MAKE UP: Press pieces under a damp cloth with a hot iron. Join side and sleeve seams using back st. Fold neckband in half to wrong side and sl-st. Press seams.

BERET

With set of four No 12 needles and A, cast on 104(112) sts. Work in rounds of k 1, p 1 rib for 1″. Change to set of four No 10 needles. **Next round:** * K 3, k into front and back of next st; rep from * to end. [130(140) sts] Cont in rounds of st-st, working rounds 1 to 3 as given on chart, noting that both sizes for Beret will beg at point marked B on chart. Work rounds 42 to 44 as given on chart. **Next round:** * K 4, k into front and back of next st; rep from * to end. [156(168) sts] Work

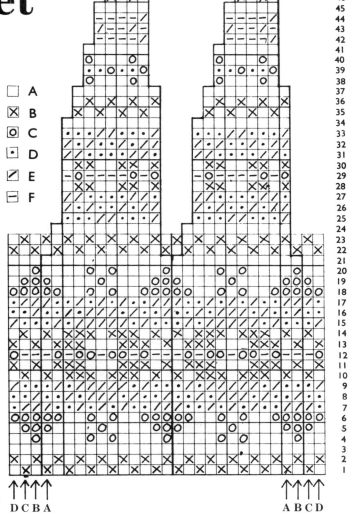

☐ A
☒ B
◨ C
⊡ D
◿ E
⊟ F

A 2nd size body; 1st size sleeves.
B 4th size body; 2nd size sleeves.
C 1st size body; 3rd size sleeves; yoke and beret.
D 3rd size body; 4th size sleeves.

rounds 38 to 41 as given on chart omitting dec on 41st round. Work rounds 1 to 33 as given on chart, shaping on rounds as given for Yoke. [117(126) sts] **Next round:** * K 3, k 2 tog, k 2, k 2 tog; rep from * 12(14) times, k 2, k 3 tog, k 2, k 2 tog(k 0). 90(98) sts. Work rounds 35 and 36 as given on chart. **Next round:** * K 1, k 2 tog; rep from * to last 0(2) sts, k 0(2). [60(66) sts] Cont working rounds 38 to 47 as given on chart, working shaping on rounds as given for Yoke. [40(44) sts] **Next round:** Break off contrast colours, with A only, * k 2 tog; rep from * to end. 20(22) sts. Break off A. Thread through sts and fasten off. Press under a damp cloth with a hot iron.

Child's military coat with beret

Instructions are for a 21″ chest. Changes for 22″, 23″, 24″ and 25″ sizes are given in brackets.

MATERIALS: Coat. 11(12-13-14-15) ozs Hayfield Beaulon Double Knitting in main shade, A; 1(1-1-2-2) ozs of same in contrast, B. **Beret.** 2 ozs of A and 1 oz of B. One pair each Nos 7, 8 and 9 needles. Ten buttons.

NOTE: For 23″ size. If making coat only, 14 ozs of A and 2 ozs of B are required. This does *not* apply if making beret too.

MEASUREMENTS: Coat. To fit a 21″(22″-23″-24″-25″) chest. Length to shoulder: 16″(18″-20″-22″-24″), adjustable. Sleeve seam: 8½″(10″-11½″-12½″-13½″), adjustable. **Beret.** To fit an average head (two sizes given).

TENSION: 11 sts to 2″ over patt on No 7 needles.

NOTE: Make Left Front first for a girl and Right Front first for a boy.

BACK: With No 8 needles and A, cast on 85(91-97-103-109) sts. Beg with a k row work 7 rows st-st. Change to No 7 needles. **Commence patt. 1st row:** [Wrong side] K 1, * y fwd, sl 1 p-wise, pass y back over sl-st, k 1; rep from * to end. **2nd row:** K 1, * k sl st and y on tog tbl, k 1; rep from * to end. These two rows form patt and are rep throughout. Cont in patt, dec 1 st at each end of 18th (20th-22nd-24th-26th) row and every foll 12th row until 69(75-81-87-93) sts rem. Cont without shaping until work measures 11″(12½″-14″-15½″-17″) from beg of patt, or required length to underarm, ending with a wrong side row. **Shape raglan.** Cast off 2 sts at beg of next 2 rows. Keeping patt correct, dec 1 st at each end of next and every foll alt row until 23(25-27-29-31) sts rem. Work 1 row. Cast off.

POCKET LININGS: [Make two] With No 7 needles and A, cast on 19 sts. Work in patt as given for Back for 24(26-28-30-32) rows. Break off yarn. Leave sts on holder.

RIGHT FRONT: Note: Buttonholes are made on Right Front for girl and Left Front for boy, working from centre front edge as follows: **Buttonhole row.** Patt 3 sts, cast off 2 sts, patt 14(16-18-20-22) sts, cast off 2 sts, patt to end. **Next row:** Patt to end, casting on 2 sts above those cast off in previous row. With No 8 needles and A, cast on 55(59-63-67-71) sts. Beg with a k row work 7 rows st-st. Change to No 7 needles. Cont in patt as given for Back, dec 1 st at end of 18th(20th-22nd-24th-26th) row and every foll 12th row, **at the same time**, when work measures 6½″ from beg of patt, make 1st set of buttonholes for girl. Cont in patt, inc as before, until work measures 7½″(8″-8½″-9″-9½″) from beg of patt, ending at front edge. ** **Insert pocket lining. Next row:** Patt 22(24-26-28-30) sts, cast off 19 sts, patt to end. **Next row:** Work in patt to cast off sts, then work in patt across 19 pocket lining sts on holder, patt to end. Cont in patt dec as before and making 2 more sets of buttonholes as markers are reached for a girl, until 8 decs in all have been worked. [47(51-55-59-63) sts] Cont without shaping until work measures same as Back to underarm, ending with a right side row. **Shape raglan.** Cast off 2 sts at beg of next row. Keeping patt correct, dec 1 st at raglan edge on next and every alt row until 30(32-34-36-38) sts rem, ending at front edge. **Shape neck. Next row:** Cast off 17(19-21-23-25) sts, patt to last 2 sts, work 2 tog. **Next row:** Patt to end. Cont in patt, dec 1 st at each end of next and every alt row until 2 sts rem. Work 1 row. K 2 tog and fasten off. Mark position for 3 sets of buttonholes on this side for a boy, first to come 6½″ from beg of patt and 2 more sets evenly spaced between, allowing for 4th set to be made in neck border.

LEFT FRONT: Work as given for Right Front, reversing shaping and making 1st set of buttonholes for a boy when work measures 6½″ from beg of patt, to **, ending with a wrong side row. **Insert pocket lining. Next row:** Patt to last 41(43-45-47-49) sts, cast off 19 sts, patt to end. **Next row:** Patt to end working across pocket lining sts on holder in place of those cast off in previous row. Complete as given for Right Front making 2 more sets of buttonholes as markers are reached for a boy and reversing all shaping. Mark position for 3 sets of buttonholes on this side for a girl, as given on Right Front.

SLEEVES: With No 9 needles and B, cast on 35(39-43-47-51) sts. Work 17 rows k 1, p 1 rib. **Next row:** K. Break off B and join in A. Change to No 7 needles. Cont in patt as given for Back, inc 1 st at each end of 12th and every foll 6th row until there are 51(55-59-65-69) sts. Cont without shaping until sleeve measures 8½″(10″-11½″-12½″-13½″) from beg, when ribbed cuff is folded in half, ending with a wrong side row. **Shape raglan.** Cast off 2 sts at beg of next 2 rows. Dec 1 st at each end of next 2 rows. Dec 1 st at each end of next and every alt row until 5(5-5-7-7) sts rem. Work 1 row. Cast off.

POCKET BORDERS: [Make two] With right side of work facing, No 9 needles and B, k up 21 sts evenly along cast off edge of pocket. Work 8 rows k 1, p 1 rib. Cast off in rib.

FRONT EDGES: With right side of work facing, No 8 needles and A, k up 71(77–83–89–95) sts evenly along Right Front edge. K 1 row. Cast off. Work Left Front edge in same way.

COLLAR: Join raglan seams using back st. With right side of work facing, No 9 needles and B, k up 25(27–29–31–33) sts up Right Front neck, 5(5–5–7–7) sts along top of sleeve, 23(25–27–29–31) sts along back neck, 5(5–5–7–7) sts along 2nd sleeve and 25(27–29–31–33) sts down Left Front neck. Work 3 rows k 1, p 1, rib making buttonholes on next 2 rows as before. Work 6 more rows k 1, p 1 rib, then work 2 buttonhole rows as before. Work 3 rows k 1, p 1 rib. Cast off in rib.

BELT: With No 9 needles and A, cast on 25 sts. Work in k 1, p 1 rib for 46(50–54–58–62) rows. Cast off in rib.

TO MAKE UP: Press work lightly on wrong side under a dry cloth with a warm iron. Join side and sleeve seams using back st. Turn hem to wrong side and sl st. Fold cuff in half to wrong side and sl st to last row of B. Fold pocket tops in half to wrong side and sl st. Neaten short ends. Fold Collar in half to wrong side and sl st. With right sides facing, fold Belt in half and join short ends turn to right side and join seam. Work buttonhole st round buttonholes. Press seams and edges. Sew on buttons and attach Belt to back with a button at each end.

BERET

With No 9 needles and B, cast on 91 (105) sts. Work 17 rows k 1, p 1 rib. **1st size only. Next row:** * Inc 1 st in first st, k 1, inc 1 st in next st, k 1, inc 1 st in next st, k 2; rep from * to last 4 sts, k 4. [129 sts] **2nd size only. Next row:** * Inc 1 st in first st, k 2, inc 1 st in next st, k 2, inc 1 st in next st, k 1; rep from * to end, inc 1 st in last st. [145 sts] **Both sizes.** Break off B and join in A. Change to No 7 needles and work in patt as given for Coat for 31(37) rows. **Shape top.** Work as given for Cap until 17(19) sts rem. Break yarn, draw through sts and fasten off.

TO MAKE UP: Press as given for Coat. Join seam. Fold rib in half to wrong side and sl st.

Baby's shawl

MATERIALS: 7 ozs of Hayfield Beaulon 3-ply fingering. One pair each Nos 7, 8 and 9 needles.

MEASUREMENTS: Approx 42" across.

TENSION: Approx 8 sts and 9 rows to 1" over lace patt worked on No 9 needles.

Begin at centre. With No 9 needles cast on 8 sts. **1st row:** Inc once in each st [16 sts] **2nd row:** As 1st. [32 sts]. **3rd row:** * P 2, y 2rn, p 2; rep from * to end. **4th row:** Counting y 2rn on previous row as 2 sts, * p 1, p 2 tog, y 2rn, p 2 tog, p 1; rep from * to end. **5th row:** As 4th. **6th row:** As 4th. [48 sts] **7th row:** * P 1, p up thread before next st [called p up 1], p 2 tog, y 2rn, p 2 tog, p up 1, p 1; rep from * to end. [64 sts] **8th row:** * P 2, p 2 tog, y 2rn, p 2 tog, p 2; rep from * to end. **9th row:** As 8th. **10th row:** As 8th. **11th row:** * P 1, p up 1, p 1, p 2 tog, y 2rn, p 2 tog, p 1, p up 1, p 1; rep from * to end. [80 sts] **12th row:** * P 3, p 2 tog, y 2rn, p 2 tog, p 3; rep from * to end. **13th row:** As 12th. **14th row:** As

12th. **15th row:** * P 1, p up 1, p 2, p 2 tog, y 2rn, p 2 tog, p 2, p up 1, p 1; rep from * to end. **16th row:** * P 4, p 2 tog, y 2rn, p 2 tog, p 4; rep from * to end. **17th row:** As 16th. **18th row:** As 16th. **19th row:** * P 1, p up 1, p 3, p 2 tog, y 2rn, p 2 tog, p 3, p up 1, p 1; rep from * to end. **20th row:** * P 5, p 2 tog, y 2rn, p 2 tog, p 5; rep from * to end. **21st row:** As 20th. **22nd row:** As 20th. Cont in this way inc on every 4th row until the foll row has been worked: * P 1, p up 1, p 17, p 2 tog, y 2rn, p 2 tog, p 17, p up 1, p 1; rep from * to end. [336 sts] **Shape sections and begin lace patt. 1st row:** * P 19, p 2 tog, y rn, p 2 tog, p 19; rep from * to end. **2nd row:** * P 18, p 2 tog, m 1, p 1, m 1, p 2 tog, p 18; rep from * to end. **3rd row:** * P 17, p 2 tog, m 1, p 3, m 1, p 2 tog, p 17; rep from * to end. **4th row:** * P 16, p 2 tog, m 1, p 1, m 1, p 3 tog, m 1, p 1, m 1, p 2 tog, p 16; rep from * to end. **5th row:** * P 15, p 2 tog, m 1, p 3, m 1, p 1, m 1, p 3, m 1, p 2 tog, p 15; rep from * to end. **6th row:** * P 14, p 2 tog, m 1, p 1, m 1, p 3 tog, m 1, p 3, m 1, p 3 tog, m 1, p 1, m 1, p 2 tog, p 14; rep from * to end. **7th row:** * P 13, p 2 tog, m 1, p 3, m 1, p 1, m 1, p 2 tog, p 1, p 2 tog, m 1, p 1, m 1, p 3, m 1, p 2 tog, p 13; rep from * to end. **8th row:** * P 12, p 2 tog, m 1, p 1, m 1, p 3 tog, m 1, [p 3, m 1, p 3 tog, m 1] twice, p 1, m 1, p 2 tog, p 12; rep from * to end. **9th row:** * P 11, p 2 tog, m 1, p 3, m 1, p 1, m 1, [p 2 tog, p 1, p 2 tog, m 1, p 1, m 1] twice, p 3, m 1, p 2 tog, p 11; rep from * to end. **10th row:** * P 10, p 2 tog, m 1, p 1, [m 1, p 3 tog, m 1, p 3] 3 times, m 1, p 3 tog, m 1, p 1, m 1, p 2 tog, p 10; rep from * to end. **11th row:** * P 9, p 2 tog, m 1, p 3, [m 1, p 1, m 1, p 2 tog, p 1, p 2 tog] 3 times, m 1, p 1, m 1, p 3, m 1, p 2 tog, p 9; rep from * to end. **12th row:** * P 8, p 2 tog, m 1, p 1, [m 1, p 3 tog, m 1, p 3] 4 times, m 1, p 3 tog, m 1, p 1, m 1, p 2 tog, p 8; rep from * to end. **13th row:** * P 7, p 2 tog, m 1, p 3, m 1, p 1, [m 1, p 2 tog, p 1, p 2 tog, m 1, p 1] 4 times, m 1, p 3, m 1, p 2 tog, p 7; rep from * to end. **14th row:** * P 6, p 2 tog, m 1, p 1, [m 1, p 3 tog, m 1, p 3] 5 times, m 1, p 3 tog, m 1, p 1, m 1, p 2 tog, p 6; rep from * to end. **15th row:** * P 5, p 2 tog, m 1, p 3, [m 1, p 1, m 1, p 2 tog, p 1, p 2 tog] 5 times, m 1, p 1, m 1, p 3, m 1, p 2 tog, p 5; rep from * to end. **16th row:** * P 4, p 2 tog, m 1, p 1 [m 1, p 3 tog, m 1, p 3] 6 times, m 1, p 3 tog, m 1, p 1, m 1, p 2 tog, p 4; rep from * to end. **17th row:** * P 3, p 2 tog, m 1, p 3, [m 1, p 1, m 1, p 2 tog, p 1, p 2 tog] 6 times, m 1, p 1, m 1, p 3, m 1, p 2 tog, p 3; rep from * to end.

18th row: * P 2, p 2 tog, m 1, p 1, [m 1, p 3 tog, m 1, p 3] 7 times, m 1, p 3 tog, m 1, p 1, m 1, p 2 tog, p 2; rep from * to end. **19th row:** * P 1, p 2 tog, m 1, p 3, [m 1, p 1, m 1, p 2 tog, p 1, p 2 tog] 7 times, m 1, p 1, m 1, p 3, m 1, p 2 tog, p 1; rep from * to end. **20th row:** * P 2 tog, m 1, p 1, [m 1, p 3 tog, m 1, p 3] 8 times, m 1, p 3 tog, m 1, p 1, m 1, p 2 tog; rep from * to end. **21st row:** P 1, * m 1, p 3, [m 1, p 1, m 1, p 2 tog, p 1, p 2 tog] 8 times, m 1, p 1, m 1, p 3, m 1, p 2 tog; rep from * ending last rep p 1. **22nd row:** * P 2, m 1, p 3 tog, m 1, p 1; rep from * to last st, p 1. **23rd row:** * P 1, p 2 tog, m 1, p 1, m 1, p 2 tog; rep from * to last st, p 1. **24th row:** P 2 tog, * m 1, p 3, m 1, p 3 tog; rep from * to last 5 sts, m 1, p 3, m 1, p 2 tog. **25th row:** * P 1, m 1, p 2 tog, p 1, p 2 tog, m 1; rep from * to last st, p 1. Change to No 8 needles and cont rep last 4 rows until work measures 16″ from centre. Change to No 7 needles and rep last 4 rows for a further 2″. **To work lace edging.** Cast on 11 sts at end of last row. Edging is worked on these sts gradually working off all sts until 11 only rem. **1st row:** Y rn, p 3 tog, [y rn, p 2 tog] 4 times, m 1, p 1, p 2 tog. **2nd row:** P 2 tog, [y rn, p 2 tog] 4 times, y rn, p 1, p 2 tog. **3rd row:** [Y rn, p 2 tog] 5 times, y rn, p 1, p 2 tog. **4th row:** P 2 tog, p 1, [y rn, p 2 tog] 4 times, y rn, p 2. **5th row:** [Y rn, p 2 tog] 5 times, y rn, p 2, p 2 tog. **6th row:** P 2 tog, p 2, [y rn, p 2 tog] 4 times, y rn, p 2. **7th row:** [Y rn, p 2 tog] 5 times, y rn, p 3, p 2 tog. **8th row:** P 2 tog, p 3, [y rn, p 2 tog] 4 times, y rn, p 2. **9th row:** [Y rn, p 2 tog] 5 times, y rn, p 4, p 2 tog. **10th row:** P 2 tog, p 4, [y rn, p 2 tog] 4 times, y rn, p 2. **11th row:** [Y rn, p 2 tog] 5 times, y rn, p 5, p 2 tog] **12th row:** P 2 tog, p 5, [y rn, p 2 tog] 4 times, y rn, p 2. **13th row:** Y rn, p 3 tog, [y rn, p 2 tog] 4 times, y rn, p 5, p 2 tog. **14th row:** P 2 tog, p 4, [y rn, p 2 tog] 5 times, p 1. **15th row:** Y rn, p 3 tog, [y rn, p 2 tog] 4 times, y rn, p 4, p 2 tog. **16th row:** P 2 tog, p 3, [y rn, p 2 tog] 5 times, p 1. **17th row:** Y rn, p 3 tog, [y rn, p 2 tog] 4 times, y rn, p 3, p 2 tog. **18th row:** P 2 tog, p 2, [y rn, p 2 tog] 5 times, p 1. **19th row:** Y rn, p 3 tog, [y rn, p 2 tog] 4 times, y rn, p 2, p 2 tog. **20th row:** P 2 tog, p 1, [y rn, p 2 tog] 5 times, p 1. These 20 rows form edging rep and are cont until only 11 sts rem. Cast off.

TO MAKE UP: Seam from centre to lace edge. Pin out to shape and press lightly with a cool iron over a dry cloth.

Bedspread

Shown on back cover

MATERIALS: Three 50-gm balls of Mahony's Blarney Bainin for each square. 59 balls will make 20 squares for a bedspread 64″ × 90″. Seven extra balls to fringe three sides of bedspread. One pair No 7 needles. Large crochet hook.

MEASUREMENTS: Each square measures 16″ × 16″ when pinned out for pressing.

TENSION: 19 sts and 30 rows measure 4″ square over background patt.

THE SQUARE: Cast on 2 sts. **1st row:** K 1, y fwd, k 1. **2nd row:** K 3. **3rd row:** K 1, y fwd, k 1, y fwd, k 1. **4th row:** K 5. **5th row:** K 1, y fwd, k 3, y fwd, k 1. **6th row:** K 7. **7th row:** K 1, y fwd, k 5, y fwd, k 1. **8th row:** K 9. Cont in background patt of 4 rows st-st, 4 rows g-st with bobbles on 3rd row of st-st bands and inc as before thus: **1st row:** K 1, y fwd, k to last st, y fwd, k 1. **2nd row:** K 1, p to last st, k 1. [11 sts] **3rd row:** K 1, y fwd, k 4, k into front, back, front, back, front of next st, turn, p 5, turn, k 5, turn, p 5, turn, sl 2nd, 3rd, 4th

and 5th sts over 1st st and k into back of bobble st [called B 1], k 4, y fwd, k 1. **4th row:** As 2nd. **5th row:** As 1st. **6th row:** K. **7th row:** As 5th. **8th row:** As 6th. Rep these 8 rows working 1 more bobble on 3rd patt row each time thus: **2nd bobble row:** [19 sts on needle] K 1, y fwd, k 5, [B 1, k 5] twice, y fwd, k 1. **3rd bobble row:** [27 sts on needle] K 1, y fwd, k 6, [B 1, k 5] twice, B 1, k 6, y fwd, k 1. **4th bobble row:** [35 sts on needle] K 1, y fwd, k 7, [B 1, k 5] 3 times, B 1, k 7, y fwd, k 1. **5th bobble row:** [43 sts on needle] K 1, y fwd, k 8, [B 1, k 5] 4 times, B 1, k 8, y fwd, k 1. After 5th bobble row, cont in patt omitting bobbles for a further 19 rows [2 rows of g-st band worked and 63 sts on needle] **63rd row:** K 1, y fwd, k 1, * y fwd, k 2 tog; rep from * to last st, y fwd, k 1. **64th row:** K. Work 6 more rows in background patt. [71 sts] **71st row:** As 63rd row. **72nd row:** As 64th row. Work 18 more rows in background patt [2 rows of st-st band worked and 91 sts on needle] **91st row:** K 1, y fwd, [k 5, B 1] 14 times, k 5, y fwd, k 1. **92nd row:** K 1, p to last st, k 1. Work 6 more rows in background patt [2 rows of st-st band worked and 99 sts on needle] Beg dec thus: **1st row:** K 1, y fwd, k 3 tog, k to last 4 sts, k 3 tog, y fwd, k 1. **2nd row:** K 1, p to last st, k 1. **3rd row:** As 1st row. **4th row:** K. **5th row:** As 3rd row. **6th row:** As 4th row. **7th row:** As 1st row. **8th row:** As 2nd row. [91 sts] **9th row:** K 1, y fwd, k 3 tog, k 2, [B 1, k 5] 13 times, B 1, k 2, k 3 tog, y fwd, k 1. **10th row:** K 1, p to last st, k 1. Work 18 more rows in background patt dec as before. [71 sts] **29th row:** K 1, y fwd, k 3 tog, k 1, * y fwd, k 2 tog; rep from * to last 4 sts, k 3 tog, y fwd, k 1. **30th row:** K. Cont to match first half, working holes on 37th row as 29th row and dec as before until 43 sts rem, then beg bobble 'Triangle' thus: **1st bobble row:** [57th row] K 1, y fwd, k 3 tog, k 5, [B 1, k 5] 5 times, k 3 tog, y fwd, k 1. **2nd bobble row:** [35 sts on needle] K 1, y fwd, k 3 tog, k 4, [B 1, k 5] 3 times, B 1, k 4, k 3 tog, y fwd, k 1. **3rd bobble row:** [27 sts on needle] K 1, y fwd, k 3 tog, k 3, [B 1, k 5] twice, B 1, k 3, k 3 tog, y fwd, k 1. **4th bobble row:** [19 sts on needle] K 1, y fwd, k 3 tog, k 2, B 1, k 5, B 1, k 2, k 3 tog, y fwd, k 1. **5th bobble row:** [11 sts on needle] K 1, y fwd, k 3 tog, k 1, B 1, k 1, k 3 tog, y fwd, k 1. After 5th bobble row cont thus: **Next row:** K 1, p 7, k 1, now cont in g-st. **Next row:** K 1, k 2 tog, k 3, k 2 tog, k 1. **Next row:** K 7. **Next row:** K 1, k 2 tog, k 1, k 2 tog, k 1. **Next row:** K 5. **Next row:** K 1, k 3 tog, k 1. **Next row:** K 3. **Next row:** Sl 1, k 2 tog, psso. Fasten off. Make 19 more squares in same way. Note that the piece will appear slightly diamond-shaped but this is rectified in pressing and joining.

TO MAKE UP: Mark out a 16″ square with four pins and stretch square to fit, pinning at each corner, then along all sides. Press on wrong side using a wet cloth and hot iron but pressing lightly to avoid flattening the bobbles. Arrange squares in four groups of four taking care to place the four cast-on corners to the centre each time. Using a finer matching yarn, backstitch just inside edges, pressing each seam as it is completed. Join the final two 'pairs' to two of the larger squares then sew main seams. For the **fringe**, cut the wool into 18" lengths and, using three strands together, knot into alternate holes at edge; space them similarly where solid g-st occurs between squares. Finally knot together three strands from one group and three strands from the next about 1" below the original knots.

Domino cushion

MATERIALS: Four balls of Mahony's Blarney Bainin for one side of cushion. Seven balls will make both sides. One pair No 7 needles; 1 cable needle. (Fabric for back of cushion if required).

MEASUREMENTS: Approx 16" square when completed.

TENSION: 9½ sts to 2" worked on g-st.

MAKE FOUR TRIANGLES ALIKE: Cast on 73 sts. K two rows. **3rd row:** K 1, sl 1, k 1, psso, k 1, * y fwd, k 2 tog; rep from * to last 3 sts, k 2 tog, k 1. **4th row:** K. **5th row:** K 1, sl 1, k 1, psso, k to last 3 sts, k 2 tog, k 1. Cont in m-st. **6th row:** K 2, * p 1, k 1; rep from * to last 3 sts, p 1, k 2. **7th row:** K 1, sl 1, k 1, psso, * k 1, p 1; rep from * to last 4 sts, k 1, k 2 tog, k 1. **8th row:** K 2, * k 1, p 1; rep from * to last 3 sts, k 3. **9th row:** K 1, sl 1, k 1, psso, * p 1, k 1; rep from * to last 4 sts, p 1, k 2 tog, k 1. **10th to 13th rows:** Rep 6th to 9th rows. **14th row:** As 6th row. This completes m-st. Work bobble band. **15th row:** K 1, sl 1, k 1, psso, k to last 3 sts, k 2 tog, k 1. **16th row:** K 2, p to last 2 sts, k 2. **17th row:** K 1, sl 1, k 1, psso, k 1, [make bobble on next st thus: k into front, back, front, back, front of next st, turn, p 5, turn, k 5, turn, p 5, turn, sl 2nd, 3rd, 4th and 5th sts over first st, k into back of bobble st—called B 1, k 4] 10 times, B 1, k 1, k 2 tog, k 1. **18th row:** As 16th. **19th row:** As 15th. Beg diamond on g-st background. **20th row:** K 25, p 2, k 1, p 2, k 25. **21st row:** K 1, sl 1, k 1, psso, k 21, sl next st on cable needle and hold at back of work, k 2, then k 1 from cable needle—called C3R, k 1, sl next 2 sts on to cable needle and hold at front of work, k 1, then k 2 from cable needle—called C3L, k 21, k 2 tog, k 1. **22nd row:** K 23, p 2, k 3, p 2, k 23. **23rd row:** K 1, sl 1, k 1, psso, k 19, C3R, k 3, C3L, k 19, k 2 tog, k 1. **24th row:** K 21, p 2, k 5, p 2, k 21. **25th row:** K 1, sl 1, k 1, psso, k 17, C3R, k 5, C3L, k 17, k 2 tog, k 1. **26th row:** K 19, p 2, k 7, p 2, k 19. Cont thus dec at each end of every right side row with 2 more sts in centre of diamond each time until the 32nd row. [43 sts]. **33rd row:** K 1, sl 1, k 1, psso, k 9, C3R, k 6, B 1, k 6, C3L, k 9, k 2 tog, k 1. **34th row:** K 11, p 2, k 15, p 2, k 11. Cont dec as before and with 2 more sts in diamond on every right side row for further 6 rows. 35 sts. **41st row:** K 1, sl 1, k 1, psso, k 1, C3R, k 6, B 1, k 7, B 1, k 6, C3L, k 1, k 2 tog, k 1. **42nd row:** K 3, p 2, k 23, p 2, k 3. Beg dec diamond. **43rd row:** K 1, sl 1, k 1, psso, C3L, k 21, C3R, k 2 tog, k 1. **44th row and every wrong side row:** K 3, p 2, k to last 5 sts, p 2, k 3. **45th row:** K 1, sl 1, k 1, psso, C3L, k 19, C3R, k 2 tog, k 1. **47th row:** K 1, sl 1, k 1, psso, C3L, k 17, C3R, k 2 tog, k 1. **49th row:** K 1, sl 1, k 1, psso, C3L, k 7, B 1, k 7, C3R, k 2 tog, k 1. [Last bobble]. Cont dec as before with 2 sts less in diamond each time until the 64th row. [11 sts], thus: **64th row:** K 3, p 2, k 1, p 2, k 3. **65th row:** K 1, sl 1, k 1, psso, sl next 2 sts on to cable needle and hold at front of work, k 1, k 2 tog, k 2 tog from cable needle, k 2 tog, k 1. **66th row:** With a No 10 needle, k 1, p 2 tog, p 1, p 2 tog, k 1, break wool leaving a few inches and leave these 5 sts on a holder.

TO MAKE UP: With right side down, pin out corners of cast-on edge 16" apart then pin all along this edge. Pin sides of triangle so that centre is 8" deep and press

Cushions

with a damp cloth and hot iron, pressing outer edges firmly but bobbles lightly. Thread wool left on last piece worked through all four sets of 5 sts, draw up tight and fasten off, neatly running in the other ends. Sew the four triangles tog and press seams. Cut fabric to fit, allowing small turnings, turn in edges and hem to wrong side of knitting along first ridge above cast on edge. Leave opening on one side to insert cushion, then stitch opening.

Leaf cushion

MATERIALS: 1 square requires 5 balls of Sirdar Sportswool. 1 pair No. 7 needles.
MEASUREMENTS: 20″ × 20″.
TO MAKE A SQUARE: With No. 7 needles cast on 3 sts. **1st row:** W on, k 3. **2nd row:** W on, k 4. **3rd row:** W on, k 2, w fwd, k 1, w fwd, k 2. **4th row:** W on, k 2, p 3, k 3. **5th row:** W on, k 3, k 1, w fwd, k 1, w fwd, k 1, k 3. **6th row:** W on, k 3, p 5, k 4. **7th row:** W on, k 4, k 2, w fwd, k 1, w fwd, k 2, k 4. **8th row:** W on, k 4, p 7, k 5. **9th row:** W on, k 5, k 3, w fwd, k 1, w fwd, k 3, k 5.

10th row: W on, k 5, p 9, k 6. **11th row:** W on, k 6, k 4, w fwd, k 1, w fwd, k 4, k 6. **12th row:** W on, k 6, p 11, k 7. **13th row:** W on, k 7, k 5, w fwd, k 1, w fwd, k 5, k 7. **14th row:** W on, k 7, p 13, k 8. **15th row:** W on, k 8, sl 1, k 1, psso, k 9, k 2 tog, k 8. **16th row:** W on, k 8, p 11, k 9. **17th row:** W on, k 9, sl 1, k 1, psso, k 7, k 2 tog, k 9. **18th row:** W on, k 9, p 9, k 10. **19th row:** W on, k 10, sl 1, k 1, psso, k 5, k 2 tog, k 10. **20th row:** W on, k 10, p 7, k 11. **21st row:** W on, k 11, sl 1, k 1, psso, k 3, k 2 tog, k 11. **22nd row:** W on, k 11, p 5, k 12. **23rd row:** W on, k 12, sl 1, k 1, psso, k 1, k 2 tog, k 12. **24th row:** W on, k 12, p 3, k 13. **25th row:** W on, k 13, sl 2 sts as if to k 2 tog, k 1, p2sso, k 13. **26th row:** W on, k 1, p to end. **27th row:** W on, k to end. **28th and 29th rows:** As 27th row. Rep 26th to 29th rows 5 times more, then 26th row once. 53 sts. **51st row:** W on, * k 2 tog, w fwd; rep from * to last st, k 1. **52nd row:** As 26th row. **53rd row:** W on, k 1, * w fwd, k 2 tog; rep from * to last 2 sts, k 2. **54th row:** As 26th row. **55th row:** As 53rd row. **56th row:** As 26th row. **57th to 59th rows:** As 27th row. **60th row:** As 26th row. **61st and 62nd row:** As 27th row. **63rd row:** W on, k 1, p 1, * w on, k 1, w rn, p 9; rep from * to last 3 sts, w on, k 1, w rn, p 1, k 1. **64th row:** W on, k 2, * p 3, k 9; rep from * ending p 3, k 3. **65th row:** W on, k 1, p 2, * k 1, w fwd, k 1, w fwd, k 1, p 9; rep from * ending k 1, w fwd, k 1, w fwd, k 1, p 2, k 1. **66th row:** W on, k 3, * p 5, k 9; rep from * ending p 5, k 4. **67th row:** W on, k 1, p 3, * k 2, w fwd, k 1, w fwd, k 2, p 9; rep from * ending p 3, k 1, instead of p 9. **68th row:** W on, k 4, * p 7, k 9; rep from * ending p 7, k 5. **69th row:** W on, k 1, p 4, * k 3, w fwd, k 1, w fwd, k 3, p 9; rep from * ending p 4, k 1, instead of p 9. **70th row:** W on, k 5, * p 9, k 9; rep from * ending p 9, k 6. **71st row:** W on, k 1, p 5, * sl 1, k 1, psso, k 5, k 2 tog, p 9; rep from * ending p 5, k 1, instead of p 9. **72nd row:** W on, k 6, * p 7, k 9; rep from * ending p 7, k 7. **73rd row:** W on, k 1, p 6, * sl 1, k 1, psso, k 3, k 2 tog, p 9; rep from * ending p 6, k 1, instead of p 9. **74th row:** W on, k 7, * p 5, k 9; rep from * ending p 5, k 8. **75th row:** W on, k 1, p 7, * sl 1, k 1, psso, k 1, k 2 tog, p 9; rep from * ending p 7, k 1, instead of p 9. **76th row:** W on, k 8, * p 3, k 9; rep from * to end. **77th row:** W on, k 1, p 8, * sl 2, k 1, p2sso, p 9; rep from * ending p 8, k 1, instead of p 9. **78th row:** As 26th row. **79th row:** As 27th row. **80th row:** As 26th row. **81st row:** As 27th row. Cast off p-wise. Break wool leaving a long end for sewing. Work 3 more pieces in same way.
TO MAKE UP: Join pieces by oversewing through the corresponding loops formed by made sts. Press. A large number of these squares can be made and joined together to form a bedspread.

Doll with clothes

MATERIALS: Doll. Three balls of Wendy Invitation Cotton in pale pink. One pair No 12 needles. Stuffing. Two blue buttons for eyes. Red felt for mouth. Small pink button for nose. One ball brown Wendy Diabolo Double Double knit for hair. **Clothes.** 2 ozs Wendy 4-ply Nylonised in main shade, A. 1 oz in contrast, B. One pair No 9 needles. Two small buttons. Shirring elastic.

MEASUREMENTS: Doll. Height: approx 15″. Body: approx 10″ round. **Dress.** Length: approx 6″.

TENSION: In cotton: 8 sts to 1″ over st-st on No 12 needles. In wool: 6 sts to 1″ over g-st on No 9 needles.

DOLL

BODY AND HEAD: [Beg at base] With No 12 needles and cotton, cast on 64 sts. Work 40 rows st-st. **Shape neck. Next row:** K 2 tog across row. [32 sts] Work 7 rows st-st without shaping. **Shape head.** Inc in each st across row. [64 sts] Work 27 rows st-st without shaping. **Shape top of head.** K 2 tog across row. P 1 row. K 2 tog across row. P 1 row. Draw thread through rem 16 sts, pull tight and finish securely.

LEGS: [Make two alike] Beg at foot. Cast on 39 sts and work 8 rows st-st. **Shape instep. 1st row:** K 18, k 3 tog, k 18. **2nd row:** P 17, p 3 tog, p 17. **3rd row:** K 16, k 3 tog, k 16. **4th row:** P 15, p 3 tog, p 15. Work 50 rows without shaping. Cast off.

ARMS: [Make two alike] Beg at hand. Cast on 16 sts. Inc 1 st at each end of next and foll 3 rows. [24 sts] Work 40 rows without shaping. Cast off.

TO MAKE UP: Fold all pieces with right sides tog. Sew centre-back of head and body and turn to right-side. Stuff head and neck firmly. Tie tape round neck to keep shape while stuffing body firmly. Sew across base from side to side. Sew sole of foot and centre back of legs. Turn right side out and stuff firmly to within ¾″ of top. With seams at back, sew each leg to half of base seam of body. Sew arm seams. Turn right side out and stuff firmly to within ¾″ of top. Gather top and sew to shoulders with seams at back. Wind a few strands of matching cotton around arm about 1½″ from end to form wrist. Tie tightly. **To make hair.** Wind brown Diabolo yarn 30 times round a 10″ card or book, slip off and tie hank tightly with matching yarn. Sew to top of head, cut loops and trim off fringe. Add features.

DRESS

BACK AND FRONT ALIKE: With B and No 9 needles, cast on 60 sts. Work 7 rows g-st. Cont in st-st working 2 rows A, 2 rows B and 30 rows A. **Next row:** [Waistband] With B, k 2 tog across row. K 1 more row with B. Break off B. Join in A and work 2¼″. Cast off.

SLEEVES: With B cast on 26 sts. K 1 row. Break off B and join in A. Work 15 rows g-st. Cast off.

TO MAKE UP: With wrong sides of work tog oversew ¼″ at outside edges of shoulders. Sew cast-off row of sleeves between B waistbands of back and front. Join underarm and side seams. Sew a button on back at each side of neck and make loops on front to fasten.

PANTS

[Make two pieces alike] With A, cast on 20 sts and work 57 rows g-st. Cast off.

TO MAKE UP: Fold one piece with cast-on and cast-off edges tog and sew ¾″ from one end. Rep with other leg. Now sew the two pieces tog to form front and back seams. Thread shirring elastic around waist.

SOCKS

[Both alike] With A cast on 30 sts. K 3 rows. Cont in g-st work 2 rows B and 30 rows A. **Next row:** K 2 tog across row. Cast off.

TO MAKE UP: Sew foot and back seam on wrong side.

Yarn conversion chart

UNITED KINGDOM	UNITED STATES	CANADA	SOUTH AFRICA	AUSTRALIA
EMU Scotch Double Knitting	*Standard double knitting	Scotch double knitting	*Standard double knitting	*Standard double knitting
HAYFIELD Beaulon 3-ply	*Standard 3-ply	*Standard 3-ply	*Standard 3-ply	*Standard 3-ply
JAEGER Summer Spun Celtic Spun	Linen yarn – no equivalent *Standard double knitting, but more yarn may be needed	Linen yarn – no equivalent *Standard double knitting, but more yarn may be needed	Linen yarn – no equivalent *Standard double knitting, but more yarn may be needed	Linen yarn – no equivalent Summer Spun
LEE TARGET Motoravia 4-ply	*Standard 4-ply	Motoravia 4-ply	Motoravia 4-ply	*Standard 4-ply
LISTER Lavenda Double Knitting	*Standard double knitting	*Standard double knitting	Lavenda Double Knitting	*Standard double knitting
MAHONY Blarney Bainin	Blarneyspun	Blarneyspun	Blarney Bainin	Blarney Bainin
PATONS Fuzzy Wuzzy Cameo Crepe Doublet	*Angora/Wool blend yarns *Standard 4-ply *Standard double double knitting	Fuzzy Wuzzy *Patons Beehive Fingering Patons Patwin 4-ply Patons Atlantic Fingering Patons Sterling Fingering *Standard double double knitting	Fuzzy Wuzzy Cameo Crepe Doublet	Fuzzy Wuzzy Bluebell Crepe *Standard double double knitting
ROBIN Crepe Double Knitting Vogue 4-ply	Crepe Double Knitting *Standard 4-ply	Crepe Double Knitting *Standard 4-ply	Crepe Double Knitting *Standard 4-ply	Crepe Double Knitting *Standard 4-ply
SIRDAR Fontein Crepe 4-ply Double Knitting Sportswool	Fontein Crepe 4-ply *Standard double knitting Nearest to Triple Knitting	Fontein Crepe 4-ply *Standard double knitting Sportswool	Fontein Crepe 4-ply Double Knitting Sportswool	Fontein Crepe 4-ply Double Crepe Sportswool
TWILLEY Crysette	Crysette or standard 4-ply	Crysette	Crysette	Crysette
WENDY Invitation Cotton 4-ply Nylonised Diabolo Double Knitting	*Standard 8's cotton *Standard 4-ply *Standard double knitting	No equivalent *Standard 4-ply *Standard double knitting	Invitation Cotton *Standard 4-ply *Standard double knitting	*Standard 8's cotton *Standard 4-ply *Standard double knitting

*These yarns are only equivalents and tension must be checked before starting work